LEARNING FROM EXPERIENCE

D0859111

SUNY Series, Teacher Preparation and Development

Alan R. Tom, editor

LEARNING FROM EXPERIENCE

MEMORY
AND THE
TEACHER'S ACCOUNT
OF TEACHING

Miriam Ben-Peretz

STATE UNIVERSITY OF NEW YORK PRESS

Published by
State University of New York Press, Albany

For information, address State University of New York
Press, State University Plaza, Albany, N.Y. 12246

Production by Dana Foote
Marketing by Fran Keneston

Library of Congress Cataloging-in-Publication Data

Ben-Peretz, Miriam.
    Learning from experience : memory and the teacher's account of
teaching / Miriam Ben-Peretz.
        p.   cm. — (SUNY series, teacher preparation and development)
    Includes bibliographical references and index.
        ISBN 0–7914–2303–4 (hc : acid-free paper).—ISBN 0–7914–2304–2
(pb : acid-free paper)
        1. Teachers—Israel—Biography.   2. Retired teachers—Israel—
Biography.   3. Experiential learning—Israel.   4. Teaching.
I. Title.   II. Series: SUNY series in teacher preparation and
development.
LA2383.I75B46   1995
371.1'0092'2—dc20
[B]   94-17215
                                                                          CIP

10 9 8 7 6 5 4 3 2 1

To the memory of my mother,
Dr. Ester Rabin,
who taught us the value
of memories and life stories.

I'm Certain I Went

I'm certain I went, out of an illusion, to look
for my footprints on a road that was covered with buildings and
                                        bordered with fences
ages ago the signs that I left were erased and even then
I knew that I wouldn't remember them something strange
                                        happened
I saw my footprints clearly engraved even
in the walls of houses the lattice of fences all
the signs shining in the dark as if anointed
phosphorous cats' eyes in the dark . . .

From *The Light of Lost Suns*
Selected Poems of Amir Gilboa
Selected and translated by Shirley Kaufman
with Shlomith Rimmon
New York, Persea Books, 1979, p. 81

CONTENTS

TABLES AND FIGURES

TABLES

FOREWORD

In *Learning from Experience: Memory and the Teacher's Account of Teaching*, Miriam Ben-Peretz advances our understanding of teachers' knowledge. She does this by addressing two principal questions: "How is experience transformed into professional wisdom?" and "What is the role of memory in this process?" We are moved forward by the reflections of retired school teachers and we are brought to a deeper, more meaningful understanding of these reflections by moving backward and focussing on the role of memory in the personal and collective construction of professional wisdom.

On receiving the invitation to write a foreword for the book, I asked Dr. Ben-Peretz what she thought to be the major contributions of the book. She replied, "The introduction of memory research into the study of teachers and teaching, the diverse ways of analyzing the recalled events, as well as some of the findings of the study." These points and their order reflect my own assessment of this book's contribution. The book presents findings that contribute to the question of how teaching experience is transformed into professional wisdom. I will note only one of the findings that particularly caught my attention and which I believe is of importance to understanding teachers' professional knowledge. But it is, indeed, the book's special focus on memory that marks this work as important and sets it apart from others in the field. Overall, my comments are directed to this aspect of the work.

First, the finding that caught my attention. The retired teachers in this study have fundamentally positive views of their professional careers. They look back with warmth, humor, and a sense of accomplishment at a lifetime of teaching. They remember the end of teaching cycles as being satisfactory moments; they remember long hours, hard work, and the satisfaction they brought; they remember individual students; they remember difficult non-homogeneous classes and the success of a curriculum struggling to serve diverse students; they remember improved student achievement perhaps, it seems, more than achievement itself; and they feel, as one teacher said, "we made a difference."

Why is this an important finding? Partially the reasons are found in Ben-Peretz's own words where she sees this aspect of the study as a kind of test of the sense, so prevalent in recent years, of teacher overload, anger, despair, and unionized resistance. As this book comes to press a world-wide economic recession is leaving its mark on government attitudes and financial support is decreasing for the social service sector. Educators at all levels, in many countries, are being asked to do the same or more with less. In my country, the school teachers in one entire province have gone out on strike and other provincial teacher federations are considering similar action. Teachers are very much in the public eye. A profession under such circumstances and marked by negative attitudes and work characteristics is jeopardized. But Ben-Peretz's retired teachers do not fit that image. Though hers is only a small-scale study, 43 teachers and 135 events collected, the findings are sufficiently interesting and provocative to warrant further studies in different national and local situations. Is this a profession under siege as is often claimed? Is it is a place we want our own daughters and sons to go for a satisfying life? Miriam Ben-Peretz's study begins to ask some of these questions. There are serious consequences for education in general, and for the lives of teacher participants, if Ben-Peretz's findings are not generalizable. She has opened the door to something in need of widespread study.

I believe that Ben-Peretz is onto something important. In the long term studies Jean Clandinin and I have pursued with beginning and experienced teachers, some of them retired, we find that it is the spirit of inquiry that drives their sense of satisfaction. Their inquiries are based not so much on successes as they are on failures, near failures, and troublesome situations. There are times when working with these teachers when one longs for a positive fantasy-filled Hollywood story to ease the tensions of coming to grips with the difficulties of teaching. Yet, like Ben-Peretz's teachers who remember "job difficulties" and "negative experiences" over "positive experiences" in a ratio of over 3:1, the ones we work with are also retrospectively dedicated and satisfaction-filled.

The juxtaposition of these two findings—the tendency to recall negative experiences on the job while also feeling satisfied—is fascinating. It implies, I think, something fundamental and quite intuitively commonsensical about the profession of teaching. It implies, as Dewey said, that a life is only lived when it is pursued educationally, by which he meant that it was lived as a narrative of inquiry, a life filled with tensions and problematic situations and with the growth that ensues from moving successfully from one inquiry to another. This juxtaposition of Miriam Ben-Peretz's findings is more telling of education and, indeed, of a way of living than are the sometimes too-easily cited reasons for teacher satisfaction. Her findings stand behind, and are at a deeper narrative level than such sources of satisfaction as love of children, the rewarding quality of a life of service and caregiving, and the sense of achievement found in professional knowledge phrases such as "the delight in watching their faces light up with understanding." Ben-Peretz's work does not deny these other sources of satisfaction. Indeed, her teachers express them. But her work challenges us to think about these matters at a more deeply biographic level.

I believe that what Ben-Peretz has put us onto reaches into the ways human beings, not only teacher professionals but all of us, lead lives of satisfaction. How can we construct a life in such a way that it is satisfying to live and satisfying to look back on? How can we plan the same things for our children and our students?

The study of memory is one important entré point to those questions. It will be one of the things for which this book is remembered. Let me say why I think this is the case. This book is positioned in a relatively new tradition of teacher studies. Teacher studies were characteristically labelled as "research on teaching" and tended to focus on teacher characteristics, processes of teaching, and the relationship of these to student achievement. More recently the terms "teacher thinking" and "teacher knowledge" have occupied research attention. Teacher thinking studies tended to evolve as combined versions of teacher characteristics and teaching processes and focused on the cognitive processes teachers used. Teacher knowledge research is an explicitly epistemological problem focused on what it is that teachers know and its relationship to what they do. The most current philosophically-based review of this research tradition is Fenstermacher's (1994) *Review of Research in Education* article, "The knower and the known in teacher knowledge research." Ben-Peretz's work is positioned within this tradition. In that tradition it is special in two ways: it focuses on retired teachers rather than preservice and inservice teachers and it explicitly raises the issue of memory and its connection to knowledge and knowing. Apart from being a fundamental philosophical matter that will, I believe, soon receive considerable attention in this research tradition, thanks in part to Ben-Peretz's work, memory represents the assumptional basis for research on teacher knowledge.

Assumptions about memory are important to teacher knowledge research. They are not so important to other aspects of research on teaching. Studies of teacher characteristics, teaching process, and their relationship to student achievement do not imply anything about memory. They are observational and correlational studies of what is. Likewise, most of the teacher thinking research has this same descriptive quality. Thinking processes are more difficult to observe and are, therefore, more conceptual in quality than are studies of teaching process. But the study of thinking processes in this research relies only modestly on memory in such methodological tactics as stimulated recall. However, many, though by no means all, studies of teachers' knowledge rely on memory. Biography, autobiography, and all forms of interview and conversation based studies such as Dr. Ben-Peretz's that rely on teacher reflections also rely on assumptions about the nature of memory. So much is this a concern in my own work with Jean Clandinin that we have begun to examine the status of memory claims in narrative studies.

The dilemma we encounter is that while memory statements are central to narrative inquiry, their epistemological status is in question. Recollections of educational events, chronicles and stories of these events, and interpretive educational narratives of life in part or in whole all rely on memory. It is memory that connects teacher knowledge studies to an empirical world and makes possible a social science of teacher knowledge. Memory connects meaning to experience for events, chronicles, stories, and narratives. There is a difference between fictional texts and empirical texts in narrative studies of teacher knowledge. Memory supplies the difference.

But what are memories relative to the experience they purport to bring forward? Memories are frequently treated as phenomenological givens, almost as if they could be touched, handled, picked up, moved around, piled here and there, and organized in various ways. In studies such as these, individual memories are like individual facts, given to the inquiry by memory collecting methods to be tabulated and interpreted. But another way of thinking about memories is as constructions pulled out of a past in which they have been repeatedly shaped by layer upon layer of experience, ever shifting nets of memories, and situations in which they are called forth. In this way of thinking, the situations in which memories are collected can make a difference to what is recalled. The memory crystalization process depends on why the memory is being recalled, by whom, and for what purpose. Interviews and conversations, such as the ones in this book in which teachers are asked to reflect on a life of teaching, are one such situation. On this view, retired teacher memories are not so much discrete, value-free data as they are elaborate, emotionally laden, intentional constructions. Some of the lines of thought behind this view of memory are reviewed by Dr. Ben-Peretz. There are important consequences for either of these assumptions about memory for the findings that one wishes to claim for studies such as this. Readers will be rewarded with added interpretive nuance by reading the findings reported in this book in the light of the chapters on the nature of memory.

This book raises the issue of memory for students of teachers and teaching at a time when studies of memory are alive in the biological and psychological literature. Last winter, for instance, Freud's work was thoroughly critiqued from the point of view of what it was that Freud's clients remembered, how he helped them remember, as well as how Freud recorded client memories. Frederick Crews' (1993) "The Unknown Freud" in *The New York Review* and Flanagan's (1993) "Memory Playing False" in the *Times Literary Supplement* are illustrative. I believe Miriam Ben-Peretz's book will mark an important moment in the assumptions made about memory in studies of teaching. The contextual intellectual climate is right for this to happen. Memory is not only a point of importance to educators working within a tradition of teacher knowledge studies but is also important in associated fields. And it is often the relationship of educational studies to its associated fields that helps drive lines of educational work forward. I believe memory signals one of those relationships and that this book will be one of its markers in educational studies.

—F. Michael Connelly
Joint Centre for Teacher Development
University of Toronto
The Ontario Institute for
Studies in Education

ACKNOWLEDGMENTS

This book is based on the professional events recalled by retired teachers. I am most grateful to the teachers who shared their memories with us for the insights they provided on the process of learning from experience.

The contribution of Sima Udovich in the analysis of the recalled events has been invaluable. Special thanks are due to Hannah Kochva who has assisted me in this study.

I am deeply indebted to Professor Richard White, Monash University, for introducing me to research on memory of events.

I wish to express my sincere gratitude to Professor Michael F. Connelly, The Ontario Institute for Studies in Education, for his encouraging and insightful remarks and for writing the foreword to this book.

For their constructive and perceptive comments on this work, I thank Professor Jean D. Clandinin, University of Alberta; Professor Charles Desforges, University of Exeter; Professor Asher Koriat, University of Haifa; and the anonymous reviewers of the manuscript.

I am particularly grateful to Professor Alan Tom, editor of this series, for his support and help.

I am deeply indebted to Lois J. Patton, editor-in-chief, and to Dana Foote, production editor, for their helpful advice, comments and support.

For their help with the statistical analyses I thank Hagai Kupermintz and Dr. Joseph Tal.

For their dedicated assistance in the difficult task of editing, typing, and proofreading, I express my gratitude and appreciation to Anat Zajdman, Joyce Sopher, and Esther Yankelevitch.

Finally, I wish to express my deep gratitude to my husband, Moshe Ben-Peretz, for his patient support throughout all stages of this work.

Introduction

Pupils are not the only ones who sometimes forget that teachers are human.
Sikes 1985, p. 57

THE IMPORTANCE OF PRACTITIONERS' STORIES

🌱 TEACHERS' life histories and narratives have begun to play a central roles in educational research. Ball and Goodson (1985b) state that "greater attention has been directed to teachers as human beings, as rounded social actors with their own problems and perspective, making careers, struggling to achieve their ideals or just struggling to 'survive' " (p. 8). Studying teachers' lives may be conceived as highly significant for understanding teachers' knowledge, as well as knowledge about teachers. Woods (1987) argues that "the life history would appear to be an eminently suitable method in the compilation of teacher knowledge. It is based within the subjective reality of the individual in a way that both respects the uniqueness of individuals and promotes identification of commonalities among them" (p. 124).

Studies of teachers' lives have been published, such as Ball and Goodson's *Teachers' Lives and Careers* (1985a), Goodson's *Studying Teachers' Lives* (1992), and Clandinin's narrative study of teacher images in action, *Classroom Practice* (1986). The linkage between teachers' knowledge and the everyday stories of teachers' lives has been documented in Schubert and Ayers's *Teacher Lore: Learning from Our Own Experience* (1992). In the prologue to their book Ayers states: "The secret of teaching is to be found in the local detail and the everyday life of teachers; teachers can be the richest and most useful source of knowledge about teaching; those who hope to understand teaching must turn at some point to teachers themselves" (p. v).

The importance of practitioners' stories in learning about one's practice has been noted, as well, in other professions.

1

Coles, who in his book *The Call of Stories* (1989) emphasizes the role of stories in the medical profession, quotes his supervisor, Dr. Williams, as having said: "Their story, yours, mine—it's what we all carry with us on this trip we take, and we owe it to each other to respect our stories and learn from them" (p. 30). Coles (1989) argues that stories are valuable in all professions where it is important to uncover meanings of human situations. The importance of "narrative inquiry" in education has been extensively argued by Connelly and Clandinin (1990). They state that "the main claim for the use of narrative in educational research is that humans are storytelling organisms who, individually and socially, lead storied lives. The study of narrative, therefore, is the study of the ways humans experience the world. This general notion translates into the view that education is the construction and reconstruction of personal and social stories; teachers and learners are storytellers and characters in their own and others' stories" (p. 2).

Real-life events of teaching and learning are segments of the "storied life" we lead as teachers; they are part of the history of practice. Stenhouse (1979) talks about history as "a critical refinement of memory" (p. 6), making experience public and opening it to dialogue. The critical refinement of memory, the public dialogue about past experiences, opens opportunities for assigning meaning to professional events.

One of the characteristics of stories is their subjectivity. Eisner (1991) argues for the virtue of subjectivity of personal biographies and unique modes of thinking. In Eisner's words, "These unique ways of experiencing make possible new forms of knowledge that keep culture viable. These new forms then become candidates for shaping the experience of others, who in turn can use them, to create even newer forms" (p. 48). Teachers, like other practitioners, learn from the stories of their experiences, which shape the wisdom of practice enacted in classrooms. The wisdom of teaching can be found in teachers' stories, which provide insights into their experiences and the knowledge and emotions that characterize their everyday professional actions.

How is experience transformed into professional wisdom? What is the role of memory in this process? These are the main questions dealt with in this book.

To gain insights into the process of learning from experience, retired teachers were asked for accounts of their former practice. Several aspects of learning from experience are treated in the various chapters of this book: (1) The nature of teachers' memories: What is the content of their recalled narratives? What are some shared characteristics of these memories? How does the context of experience shape teachers' memories? (2) The structure of teachers' narratives: the "grammar" of their stories, their themes and plots, their style and language. (3) The manner in which teachers transform concrete experiences into practical wisdom: How are rules and principles of practice formulated and presented? (4) What do teachers' stories tell us about teachers and teaching? Several of the recalled events are reproduced in different chapters, serving as foci for diverse analyses.

We assumed that retired teachers had reached the peak of their professional knowledge and had gained insights into the process of becoming experts at their craft. Retired teachers could look back over many years of practice, and their choices of past events provided a view of changing educational situations. The participating teachers were eager to share their stories, freed from the stress of everyday teaching demands. The author of this book was the principal researcher assisted by two research assistants, Hannah Kochva and Sima Udovich.

The collection of stories of retired teachers in Israel provides a mode of reconstructing the history of practice over time. The professional cases produced by veteran teachers can be valuable in stimulating novice teachers' reflection on their work. This book, then, concerns the general issue of recall of autobiographical professional events and the ways in which teachers organize and retrieve their past experiences.

OVERVIEW OF CHAPTERS

Chapter 1 introduces some central concepts and theories in the realm of memory of events, discussing these in the context of teaching. Distinctions between episodic and semantic memory are presented, and the nature of autobiographical memory is defined. Several themes concerning the structure of memory

are discussed, such as scripts and memory organization packets (MOPs). The chapter deals with issues of recall, expert knowledge, the effects of age on memory, and the contents of
autobiographical memory, and it closes with a description of
the manner in which memories of retired teachers were collected. The events were presented by the participants in Hebrew
and were translated by the author.

Chapter 2 is devoted to the presentation and discussion of
teacher memories. Content categories are defined and exemplified. Based on quantitative analyses, some shared characteristics of memories are noted and discussed.

A major part of chapter 3 deals with the impact of teaching contexts on teacher memories. The term *context* in this
study referred to the type of teacher (kindergarten or school),
the period of the event, and the socioeconomic level of the
student population. Several content categories of memories were
found to be significantly different in different contexts. The
chapter examines the affective quality of teachers' memories in
relation to the teachers' tenure characteristics. Finally, teachers' views about factors determining recall are reviewed.

Chapter 4 examines lesson scripts of retired teachers.
Scripts are conceived as representing generalizations of past
experiences that serve as guides for further action. The chapter
identifies several common elements, as well as individual components, of scripts and discusses the analogy between teacher
scripts and teacher routines.

Chapter 5 is devoted to a detailed analysis of several recalled events. The main question dealt with in this chapter is
what the participating teachers have learned about themselves,
their students, and the schools they used to work in. Special
attention is paid to the overall tone of professional satisfaction
evident in the stories of retired teachers.

Chapter 6 deals with the structure of teachers' stories, the
"point of view" reflected in the recalled events, and the stylistic
characteristics of the texts. The coherence of stories is examined according to various organizing principles, such as chronological or causal connections. Regarding points of view, a
distinction is made between an observer's perspective and one's
own "field perspective." The lack of use of professional terms by
teachers is noted and discussed.

Chapter 7 treats different conceptions of the relationship between experience and professional knowledge. This chapter compares teaching with other professions with respect to the role experience plays in becoming professionals. The chapter discusses "reframing" as a possible mode for developing professional knowledge and presents ways of linking event knowledge and organized taxonomic knowledge.

Teachers' views about learning from experience are the focus of chapter 8. This chapter discusses the emerging themes of learning from experience in statements of retired teachers. The process of "collective remembering" is an important aspect of learning from experience; this chapter compares studies of learning from experience in different teaching contexts with the findings in this study.

Chapter 9 presents some conclusions, focusing on context-specific memories, on the moral nature of teachers' recalled events, and on the synergetic effect of sharing one's experiences, and presents the notion of secondary functionality of events and its role in retrieval.

Chapter 10 deals with some possible implications for teacher education and school administration, including several ways to use teachers' recollected stories and scripts and the importance of providing administrative opportunities for collective remembering.

This is a book about recollected events in the lives of retired teachers in Israel. Their stories provide opportunities for listening to their voices and learning about their experiences. Maxine Greene (1991) talks about the sounds of storytelling being everywhere today. She marvels at the richness of multiple voices, "the sound of many discourses, many voices; and the consciousness of a listener or reader affecting what is thought and what is said" (p. x).

As a teacher of biology in high school, as well as a teacher educator, I had many opportunities to reflect on my past experiences, to give meaning to these experiences, to define myself as a person and as a teacher, and to share my stories with colleagues and students. I became aware that knowledge may be embodied in our narratives, and I wanted to learn more about the nature of teachers' narratives, about their learning from experience, and about the manner in which memory shapes

their stories. Thanks to many retired teachers' generous sharing of their recollections, this book came to be. Before turning
to their stories, let me share with you one of my own. This
event happened in my first year of teaching biology in a junior
high school. Previously I had some experience of teaching in an
elementary school. As grades 7 through 9 had only a limited
number of biology lessons, I was assigned to teach all three
grade levels. This meant that I had to spend many hours pre-
paring lessons on different topics for varied age levels. I still
remember the enormous load of grading the tests of about two
hundred students. Still, I was enthusiastic about my work and
I decided that at the end of the year we would set up an
exhibition reflecting our yearlong studies. The students cooper-
ated eagerly and ingeniously. Posters were planned and pre-
pared. Models were built, plants and animals were collected
and exhibited. It was a beautiful exhibition, well received by
fellow students, parents, and colleagues. For me this was a
turning point. I learned about the manifold ways of acquiring
knowledge. Above all, I had experienced the rewards of teaching. My professional identity had been defined—I had become a
teacher. Since that joint enterprise, I have come to view my
students at all ages and levels, and in all contexts, as full
partners in the teaching-learning process.

Let us turn now to the recollections of retired teachers.

1

Memory of Events and the Practice of Teaching

To study a subject best—understand it thoroughly before you start.
> Finagle's Rule for Scientific Research (Dickson 1978, p. 58)

🌿 EVERYDAY events and incidents become part of our memory and can determine to a large extent our behavior in diverse situations. Neisser (1982a) contends that "everyone uses the past to define themselves. Who am I? I have a name, a family, a home, a job. I know a great deal about myself: what I have done, how I have felt, where I have been, whom I have known, how I have been treated. My past defines me, together with my present and the future that the past leads me to expect" (p. 13). Neisser argues the importance of studying how people use their past experiences to deal with present and future situations. The use of past experiences may be perceived as a central feature of private and professional actions.

In professional contexts, one might be required to predict a future event or to explain a past event. "In both cases, people may actively attempt to organize the information they received in a way that permits it to be understood in terms of a previously formed event schema" (Wyer and Scrull 1989, p. 247).

Professional memories can be conceived as constituting a central part of the wisdom of practitioners, with the potential of serving the individual, as well as his or her peers. In utilizing this wisdom, one relies on memories of past events. Memory of events is conceived herewith as providing the basis for the construction and organization of teachers' personal professional knowledge in a way that will allow them to use this knowledge.

7

The study of teachers' professional memories is, therefore, important for understanding the development of the wisdom of practice. In Neisser's words: "Everybody who is skilled at anything necessarily has a good memory for whatever information that activity demands. Physicists can remember what they need to know to do physics, and fishermen what they need for fishing; musicians remember music, art critics recall paintings, historians know history. Every person is a prodigy to his neighbours, remembering so much that other people do not know. We should be careful in what we say about memory in general until we know more about these many memories in particular" (Neisser 1982a, p. 17).

What are some insights about memory that can inform the study of teachers' professional memories? The following sections present some basic concepts in relation to teachers' memories and the context of teaching.

EPISODIC, AUTOBIOGRAPHICAL, AND SEMANTIC MEMORY

Cohen (1989), consolidating an impressive array of research concerning everyday memory, notes the basic distinction between episodic and semantic memory made by Tulving (1972). According to Tulving, episodic memory consists of personal experiences stored as information about episodes or events; these memories are context bound and refer to specific times and spaces, and to relations among events. Semantic memory, on the other hand, consists of general knowledge about the world that is organized in schemas or categories and is context free; its retrieval does not usually involve the experience of remembering. Cohen (1989) makes an important point that is highly relevant for the study of teachers' memory: "The two forms of knowledge are not separate compartmentalised structures but are in an interactive and interdependent relationship. Semantic knowledge is derived from episodic memories by a process of abstraction and generalisation" (pp. 114–15).

In other words, episodic memory about specific events, based on personal experience, can be transformed into generalized knowledge about the objective reality of the world. The issue of this transformation in the context of teaching will be examined later on.

If we accept the definition of episodic memory as concerning the memory of past personal events, we may view it as being equivalent to autobiographical memory. According to Cohen (1989), "Autobiographical memories are episodes recollected from an individual's past life" (p. 117).

Robinson (1986) speaks about autobiographical memory as "the memories a person has of his or her own life experiences" and argues that "life memories tell us something about remembering and about the rememberer" (p. 19). The study of teachers' memories of their professional life seems an appropriate endeavor for learning about memory and remembering, as well as for learning about teachers, the rememberers, and their work.

Teachers' work consists of a chain of both routine and unusual experiences. Over time, experiences become recollections of particular episodes in the past. Brewer (1986) argues that personal memories appear to be a "reliving" of experiences, at specific times and locations, accompanied by reports of visual imagery, thoughts, and felt affect. It is interesting to note that personal memories may be considered by the rememberer to be a true record of the originally experienced event, though this is not necessarily the case. In the following chapters it will be shown how the personal memories of retired teachers demonstrate the features of visual imagery and felt affect.

Conway, in his book *Autobiographical Memory* (1990), characterizes autobiographical memories as being high in self-reference and personal interpretation, having variable veridicality, and being accompanied by context-specific sensory and perceptual attributes and, frequently, imagery.

THE STRUCTURE OF MEMORIES

Researchers in the memory domain postulate that memory is not amorphous and cannot be perceived as an undifferentiated mass of remembered items. Scholars propose different structural systems for organizing memories. Cohen (1989) sums up some of the findings as follows:

> The consensus of the findings indicates that organisation is predominantly categorical, with types of events or actions being represented at different levels

of generality/specifity. When people try to recall a particular episode from the past, retrieval processes access the level of categorisation that provides the optimum context for search. This optimum level of categorisation is one that is rich and specific enough to generate useful cues and reminders. Particular episodes that are sufficiently distinctive, novel, deviant, or recent are not absorbed into generalised representations but are represented at the most specific level where they can be identified by specific tags. (p. 128)

Other organizational schemas are possible, such as the array of memories along a time line, or in terms of persons one knows (Brewer 1986).

Neisser (1986) sees similarity between the uses of the concept of "nesting" in ecological descriptions of the real world and its uses in understanding the structure of memories. Things are components of other things without any clear hierarchy because of the many transitions and overlaps. The nested structure of memories may play a crucial role in their recall. "There are links between the levels: When one of them becomes active in recall I can recall others that are nested inside it, or in which it is nested. Most recall moves either downwards from context or upwards from particulars" (p. 77). Neisser's ecological theory of nested autobiographical memory might have implications for the study of teachers' memories and might serve to explain teachers' individual styles of recall—downward from context, or upward from particulars.

We shall see, later on, that generality versus specificity as well as chronological or interpersonal organizational schemes, can be discerned in the recollected events provided by retired teachers.

SCRIPTS

Not all personal memories are specific; some are generic personal memories. According to Brewer (1986), "Repeated exposure to a set of related experiences can give rise to a generic image of the experiences" (p. 30).

Brewer's description of "generic personal memories" is close to the notion of "script"—representing knowledge about events and experiences acquired over time (Schank and Abelson 1977). Cohen (1989) defined a script as "a general knowledge structure which represents the knowledge abstracted from a class of similar events, rather than knowledge of any one specific episode. A script consists of a sequence of actions which are temporally and causally ordered and which are goal directed" (p. 110).

People are conceived of as acquiring manifold scripts for familiar experiences, like going shopping. Scripts are guidelines for understanding life events; they provide a framework for remembering events and for acting upon these memories. Scripts can be enormously important in daily life. According to Cohen (1989), memory for personal experiences "provides us with a store of 'recipes' for handling current problems and current situations. We know how to behave in social and professional contexts, how to cope with practical problems like changing the wheel on a car, or booking tickets for the theatre, because we remember how it worked out last time we had a similar experience" (p. 109).

What can we learn from the notion of "script" to account for the wisdom of teachers as practitioners? How are scripts related to teachers' routines (Leinhardt, Weidman, and Hammond 1987)? These questions will be dealt with in chapter 4.

Recent developments of the script model have been suggested by Schank (1982), who concludes that memories can be organized at different levels of generality. Memory is conceived as dynamic, allowing for constant reorganization of memory structures in light of changing requirements. Common elements may be represented in memory at a more general level and can be incorporated into diverse scripts when required. In teachers' practice, generalized actions can include, for instance, "managing classroom order and quiet," which can be incorporated into the script "giving a test" or "quiet reading time."

Schank (1982) has suggested even more general representations. These are general themes that may serve to organize memory of events, such as the theme "success." Themes allow us to recognize similarities between seemingly different events. The theme "success" might come into mind while one is trying to increase student motivation. One might be reminded of one's own lack of motivation to learn skiing, and of the impact of gradual successes on one's readiness to devote time and effort to this endeavor.

Scripts, general elements, and themes do not exist in a vacuum; they are determined by the social context, as well as by one's personal history. In the case of teachers' professional memories, "social context" is to be understood as pertaining to the culture of schools, the culture of teaching, and the wider cultural frame in which teachers live. The impact of context on teachers' memories is dealt with in chapter 3.

If we accept the basic premise that professional knowledge depends to a large extent on memory of past events, we must ask ourselves what are the factors determining recall.

FACTORS INFLUENCING RECALL

Everyday wisdom presents us with contradictory statements concerning recall. It is sometimes claimed that if you can't remember something, it couldn't have been important. On the other hand, some declare that we always remember best the irrelevant. What does research on memory have to say about factors influencing recall?

The issue of recall of personal memories has interested a number of researchers. Brewer (1986) summarizes the findings regarding the characteristics of events that are well recalled. These characteristics are uniqueness (Linton 1979; White 1982), consequentiality (Rubin and Kozin 1984), unexpectedness (Linton 1979; Rubin and Kozin 1984), and being emotion-provoking (White 1982; Rubin and Kozin 1984). Conversely, poor recall results from events that are repeated or trivial (Linton 1975).

According to Brewer (1986), the development of generic personal memories comes at the expense of individual personal memories. Therefore it is more difficult to remember any one event if it is an example of a series of similar occurrences.

We'll find that teachers tend to remember unique experiences in their past, as well as events that were highly consequential for their practice. An interesting question concerns the affective nature of teachers' memories. Do teachers tend to recall and recount more pleasant than unpleasant events? Research on memory of events tells us that pleasant events are remembered better than unpleasant or neutral events (Wagenaar 1986). Wagenaar's study corroborates Linton's (1986) finding concerning the rarity of "negative" memories. Professional memories might not exhibit this trait of omitting unpleasant events, probably because of the different framing of recall. It may be important for professionals to remember failures as well as successes, as guides for further action.

Interesting findings for the purpose of the present study are those of Rubin and Kozin (1984), who asked students to describe three of their clearest memories, rating these for the following characteristics: national importance, personal importance, surprise, vividness, emotionality, and how frequently they had discussed them. The most often mentioned events concerned injuries, sports, and meetings with the opposite sex. The vividness of memories correlated with their rated importance, degree of surprise, and emotionality. It seems that traumatic and uniquely significant experiences tend to leave stronger traces in memory. Teachers' memories reflected this tendency. Many of their stories are vivid descriptions of traumatic or other significant past experiences.

According to Reiser, Black, and Kalamanides (1986), "To find an event in memory, it is necessary to construct a plausible scenario for that event's occurrence, thus using essentially the same mechanisms necessary to understand the original event. Retrieval is therefore a process of reunderstanding the experience" (p. 101). This approach to memory provides a possible insight into the link between teachers' past experiences and their future actions. Every time teachers rely on their past professional experiences to solve present problems, the very act of retrieval constitutes a process of reflection and "reunderstanding," thus enabling the rememberer to act deliberately and appropriately in the new situation.

EXPERT KNOWLEDGE AND
THE ROLE OF MEMORIES

It was stated above that memory is the basis of action in social and professional contexts. How, then, do experts and novices differ regarding the realm of memory? Cohen (1989) claims that "when someone ceases to be a novice and becomes an expert in some particular knowledge domain, changes which are both qualitative and quantitative have taken place in the knowledge structures stored in memory" (p. 162). Some of these changes are considered to be similar in different areas of expertise. Experts know more than novices, but they are also more able to acquire and retain new information. McCloskey and Bigler (1980) argue that experts are better than novices at organizing stored knowledge into subsets. Cohen (1989) summarizes existing research in different knowledge domains that confirms that expert knowledge is more highly organized than novice knowledge. Expertise does not improve your memory in general; experts only have "better memories for meaningful properly structured information in their particular knowledge domain" (p. 164).

Fivush and Slackman (1986) found that older children are able to flexibly reorganize their event knowledge to meet the demands of changing tasks. Younger children, on the other hand, can use their event knowledge only in canonical form. This finding may be helpful for understanding the differences between expert and novice teachers. Novice teachers may tend to use their limited event knowledge concerning teaching situations in the same way that young, inexperienced children use their event knowledge. With the growth and elaboration of their "teaching scripts," expert teachers, like older children, may be able to reorganize their event knowledge in appropriate ways to match changing classroom situations.

One of Linton's (1986) interesting findings in her longitudinal autobiographical memory study was that when classifying her memories into two major themes—professional/work and social/self-centered—she found that all professional/work items were recalled before any social/self-centered items were. This finding may be interpreted as demonstrating the centrality of professional memories in one's self-schema. The study of teachers' memories of their professional lives is based on the assumption that professional memories are, indeed, highly significant in teachers' lives and that the study of their retrieval can provide insights into the complexities of teachers' expertise. Such a study raises the issue of the veridicality of memories of events. Theories of memory differ in their approach to this issue.

THEORIES ABOUT MEMORIES

Two dominant theories of memory are the copy theory and the theory of reconstructive memory. According to the first approach, personal memories are copies of earlier experiences—"a direct vision of the genuine past" (Earle 1956, p. 10). Brewer (1986) claims that copy theories were adopted for three reasons: a view of memory as based on the fading of original sensation, and a strong belief in the accuracy of one's personal memories, and the fact that personal memories include irrelevant details.

Recent studies have provided evidence that contradicts the assumptions of copy theories of personal memories, suggesting instead that memories are nonveridical reconstructions of earlier experiences (Linton 1982; Neisser 1982b). This evidence is based on gaps between recorded memories and the original event. Moreover, Nigro and Neisser (1983) found that personal memories may be reported from the perspective of an observer and not from the perspective of the individual who had experienced the event originally, and that therefore these memories could not be copies of the original perceptions of the person remembering the event.

Neisser (1986) claims that

> recall is almost always constructive. No matter how well you remember an event, the information available will not specify all the context that once gave it meaning, or all the molecular actions that were nested inside it. If you care to try, you can build on what remains to reconstruct some of what is missing. How much you make up and how much you are content to omit will depend on your situation at the time of recall and on your intention. . . . Perhaps the smallest amount of elaboration takes place when you are remembering silently for your own purposes; more appears as soon as you offer an overt account to another person. (p. 78)

Neisser's position denies the possibility of complete copy memories because of the complexity and richness of each experienced event, which is not specified during recall and has to be reconstructed by the rememberer.

Brewer (1986) tries to reconcile between the two opposing approaches and argues for a "partial reconstructive view." Brewer argues that because perceptions are not always veridical with respect to reality, one cannot assume that personal memories are uninterpreted copies of one's perceptions. Yet Brewer proposes that more-recent memories are, in fact, "reasonably accurate copies of the individual's original phenomenal experience" (p. 43). On the other hand, Brewer states that "scheme-based reconstructive processes occur in many forms of memory and there is no reason to believe that personal memory is isolated from these memory processes. One might expect that childhood memories that have been recalled and discussed a number of times would be strong candidates for reconstructive processes" (p. 43). He concludes that "with time, or under strong schema based processes, the original experience can be reconstructed to produce a new nonveridical personal memory that retains most of the phenomenal characteristics of other personal memories (e.g. strong visual imagery, strong belief value)" (p. 44). This process of reconstruction explains the fact that even memories of long ago carry the flavor of recency of experience. This "flavor of recency" is highly pronounced in the recollected professional events of teachers.

What does this controversy mean for the study of teachers' memories? Because of the background of the participants in this study, all of whom were retired professionals, none of the collected memories were recent. So we may safely assume that the process of reconstruction has shaped their stories. Still, their memories are perceived in this study as reflecting real and significant events. As Neisser (1986) states: "We remember the moment when we first heard that Kennedy has been shot because it links us to a historical occasion. The same principle probably applies to most of our vivid and well-preserved memories, though their significance is usually personal rather than political" (p. 79).

In chapter 3 we shall see that the choice of remembered events by teachers, and the vividness of their recall, can be explained on the basis of personal, as well as social, significance. Though autobiographical material may not be quite accurate, it does reflect the integrity of one's life.

EFFECTS OF AGE

Because all the respondents in the present study were retired teachers, it is important to deal with possible age effects on their processes of retention and retrieval. A number of studies show common basic patterns in recall: namely, a childhood amnesia component for the earliest years of one's life; a simple retention component for the most recent twenty to thirty years, with the mean number of memories declining as a function of age; and a reminiscence component for people older than thirty-five. Reminiscence consists of a peak of memories during the ages of about ten to thirty. In Franklin and Holding's study (1977), all fifty-, sixty-, and seventy-year-olds showed reminiscence in the ten- to thirty-year-old range. Cohen and Faulkner (1988) showed that this peak concerned highly significant life events, which tend to occur during this time of life.

We may assume, therefore, that the respondents in our study were at an age of reminiscence, an age in which some kind of life review takes place. Because they were requested to record only their professional memories, they tended to focus on their first years of practice, when they were about twenty to thirty years old and were likely to have experienced highly significant professional developments.

CONTENTS OF AUTOBIOGRAPHICAL MEMORY

Memory of past events is assumed to guide future actions. Therefore it is deemed important to ask about the content of teachers' memories. Linton (1986) claims that there is much to be learned from the survey of the contents of memory. From the point of view of teachers' memories it is important to know which memories tend to survive, what forms they take, and how they shape teachers' professional actions. Studies of their personal histories show the importance of preservice teachers' critical experiences in their past (Knowles and Holt-Reynolds 1991). Student-teachers' experiences as students may constitute negative, as well as positive, examples of teaching. According to Knowles and Holt-Reynolds (1991), "These stories or vignettes, for that is the form in which such memories are retold, comprise an essential foundation for preservice teachers' knowledge of classrooms, teachers, students and instruction, which they then use to think about the potential value of ideas they encounter in course work as they develop knowledge about teaching" (p. 91).

Kelchterman (1991) found that some past experiences were perceived by teachers as having crucial influence on their self and on their professional behavior. Such experiences can be called "critical incidents." Kelchterman states that they "are often described as very detailed anecdotes with an exemplary, illustrative, legitimate or explanatory function" (p. 7).

In different studies concerning the teaching profession, critical experiences, incidents, persons, or phases are the cornerstones of the contents of professional memories. The overall mood of these personal memories may be either positive or negative. This phenomenon contradicts Linton's (1986) finding that "the contents of memory as represented by the recall protocols are curiously silent about specific negative events" (p. 59).

It may be that this is a salient difference between professional memories, which include the negative aspects of events, and purely personal ones, which tend to overlook them. Still, Woods (1987) emphasizes the positive aspects of teachers' memories and states that "as well as facilitating expression, therefore, the life history permits a celebration of the self, and enhancement of the primary rewards of teaching" (p. 128). Many of the stories told by retired teachers may be viewed as being about "critical incidents." These incidents may refer to past negative, and even traumatic, experiences; alternatively, some stories seem to celebrate teachers' successes and the rewards of teaching.

STORIES IN AUTOBIOGRAPHICAL MEMORY

Of special importance for the present study is an approach to autobiographical memories as "stories." Stories are, as Elbaz (1991) argues, "that which most adequately constitutes and presents teachers' knowledge" (p. 3). This approach explains some of the contents to be found in accounts of memories. As Robinson (1986) has noted, "From the beginning biographers and historians have used personal recollections to construe the individual and collective past. . . . According to this view, life memories are time capsules, records of an unrepeatable past. As such they can be used both to recount the past and to teach lessons for the future. The intimate association between memory and narrative arises from this urge to use the past to instruct present and future generations" (p. 19).

The narrative form has been shown to shape the recollection of memories. Brown and Kulik (1977) content that "flashbulb" memories, which are extremely vivid and detailed, have a canonical structure that includes the following components: location, activity, source, affect, and aftermath. According to Neisser (1982b), these are the product of "narrative conventions" that govern the format of storytelling. Barclay (1986) reports on a study in which the subjects were asked to use a format derived from "story grammar" (Stein and Goldman 1979) to record three memorable events a day, for five days each week, for four months. The format included the following components: context, description of the event, and the emotional and behavioral reaction to or evaluation of the event. We shall see that this story grammar can be found as well in teachers' recollections of professional events.

The notions of "story grammar" or "narrative conventions" do not suffice to portray the complexities and richness of autobiographical memories. A more in-depth view is provided by Howarth (1980), who suggests that autobiographies may take one of three forms: oratory, drama, and poetry. Oratory form is normative in theme and didactic in purpose, and it presents some rules of conduct. In the dramatic form, the authors dramatize their story as they tell the events of their life in great detail. The poetic form does not convey ideological messages, nor does it portray "life on a stage." Rather, the author communicates her or his search for meaning and involves the reader in this search.

Teachers' personal professional memories may reflect these different autobiographical forms, shaping the content and form of their stories.

COLLECTING TEACHERS' MEMORIES

The research presented in this book is about everyday memory based on teachers' introspection, the professional memories of a sample of retired teachers. The recorded events are highly meaningful to the participants in the study. Data was collected by the researchers in familiar settings, such as a common room in the university or private homes, and not in laboratory settings. Almost all material was collected orally. This method was chosen because of the great difficulty of obtaining written responses. Moreover, the oral mode was considered more appropriate for telling one's story. The stimulus question was this: "What can you tell me about recollected events of your teaching practice?" The number, content, and format of events was left open so as not to limit the process of retrieval. The flow of the stories was not interrupted by additional questions, so as not to influence the stories in any way. Teachers' words were recorded verbatim. Forty-three teachers participated in the study. Altogether 135 events were collected; of these, 17 were submitted in writing. The proportion of schoolteachers and kindergarten teachers who had submitted their recollections in writing was about equal to their proportion in the participating group.

The question itself was meaningful to all respondents. Because of its link to the personal history of the retired teachers, it is difficult to document the validity of responses. Yet because of the nature of recorded events, which tended to relate to historical events and concrete contexts of the educational system, the ecological validity of teachers' stories could be corroborated by the researchers.

Further data was collected through lengthy and repeated interviews with fifteen teachers. Most interviews were conducted individually or in small groups. It is interesting to note that all teachers participated in the study with great enthusiasm. They enjoyed the opportunity to relate past experiences and to share their stories and insights with others.

Fifteen retired teachers provided detailed scripts of lessons and discussed the determinants of memorability. One of the major topics of interest in these discussions was the nature of professional knowledge, its development over time, and the role of experience in its growth.

THE RETIRED TEACHERS' BACKGROUND

Who are the participants in the study of teachers' professional memories? Of the forty-three teachers who participated in the study, eleven were kindergarten teachers, twenty-nine were elementary school teachers, two were high school teachers, and one had taught in a teacher education college. Of the former high school teachers, one was male, all others were female, reflecting the predominance of women in preschool and elementary educational establishments. Twenty-six of the participants were educated in teacher education colleges. One kindergarten teacher, nine elementary school teachers, two high school teachers, and the teacher-education-college teacher, had earned a B.A. degree. Four elementary teachers had the M.A. All had teaching certificates issued by the Ministry of Education. They had taught in various locales. Twenty-three teachers had taught only in cities. Seven had taught in villages, two on a kibbutz. Six related stories of their experiences in small development towns that were inhabited mainly by immigrants. Five teachers recalled events that had occurred while they were teaching in temporary camps that housed newcomers to the country. The narrators tended to choose those sites in which they started out as teachers, sites that constituted the background for the unfolding drama of their early experiences.

SUMMARY COMMENTS

This chapter presents some central concepts and theories, concerning memory of events and autobiographical memory, that are relevant to teachers' professional memories: episodic and semantic memory, scripts and their role in human action, the structures of memory of events, and the processes of retrieval and recall. The copy theory of memory was compared with the reconstruction theory. Possible relationships between the nature of autobiographical memory and the professional development of teachers were considered. The narrative mode of autobiographical memories was emphasized.

In the following chapters we will pursue several aspects of professional memories and their links to the growth of teachers' personal knowledge.

2

The Content of Teachers' Memories

When I was younger I could remember anything,
whether it had happened or not; but my faculties are
decaying now, and soon I shall be so I cannot remember any but the things that never happened.
    Mark Twain, *Autobiography*

❧ NOW we will take a look at the content of teachers' memories, highlighting some shared characteristics of their memories and the distinctive ways in which the social and historical context shapes these memories. This discussion will rely on quantitative analyses, which were conducted at several levels.

LEVELS OF ANALYSIS

This and the following chapters use several levels of analysis, from macro to micro. The macro level is that of the teacher, of which there were forty-three in the study. One level lower are events. An event is defined as an account containing a description of an incident or a chain of related incidents; 135 events were collected. At a further microlevel we find references. A reference is an allusion, in one or more sentences, to a particular topic within one event. Consequently, there may be a number of different reference topics in each event. The reference topics were classified as content categories. Altogether, eight content categories were identified: focus on students, interpersonal relationships, rules and principles, negative experiences, teaching alternatives, situation background, job difficulties, and positive experiences. These categories are described in detail later in this chapter. References are viewed as quantitative indicators of emphasis. Presumably, the more often a topic is referred to, the more it stands out in teachers' memories.

23

Several categories were further subdivided. Subcategories of interest were compared between school and kindergarten teachers. In two instances significant differences emerged for the subcategories. This is especially intriguing where no differences were found at higher levels of analysis.

The reliability of reference categories was determined as follows: Two raters independently categorized 260 of 280 references into the eight categories (20 references were used for practice). Kappa for the two raters was .96.

STATISTICAL ANALYSES

The statistical analyses are based on chi-square statistics that compare the prominence of content categories. These categories were cross-tabulated with

a. Type of teacher (kindergarten or school)
b. Event period (time of occurrence of event)
c. Type of student population (socioeconomic level)

These background variables were conceived as possibly having an impact on the nature of teachers' experiences and on their professional memories. Further details concerning the nature of the statistical analyses used in the study can be found in the appendix.

Before turning to a discussion of the content of teachers' memories, let us consider briefly the timing of the recalled events.

TIMING OF RECALLED EVENTS

An interesting finding is that the teachers in this study tended to date their memories (e.g., "my first year of teaching"), though they were not explicitly required to do so.

About half of all recalled events occurred in the retired teachers' first years of practice (years 1–10). Presumably these were the years that shaped their professional identity. Of these, sixty events (75%) took place during the first five years; 40 percent took place during the first year. (See table 1 for the data concerning the timing of events, as well as the level of schooling referred to.)

Table 1. Temporal Distribution of Autobiographical Professional Memories (number of events)

		SCHOOL TYPE			
	Kindergarten	Elementary School	High School	Teacher Education College	Total
Years of Practice at Time of Event					
1	8	16			24
2–5	9	12			21
6–10	4	11			15
11–15	5	13		1	19
16–20	4	8	4	2	18
21–25	8	10			18
26–30	4	6	3		13
31–35	6	1			7
Total number of events	48	77	7	3	135

This finding is congruent with research on memory of events, which shows that people tend to recall first impressions and incidents of primary importance in their lives.

THE CONTENT OF TEACHERS' RECOLLECTIONS

What were the most frequent content categories in the teachers' memories, and how do these reflect the salient experiences of their past?

Researchers on memory of everyday events have been interested in the content of autobiographical memories. Linton (1986), for instance, asked herself what memories survive and thrive over time. She noticed that rewriting does occur, and the work of the "internal historian" can be detected. Linton notes the role of salience of events in the retrieval process. It seems that the perceived importance of events, their emotionality, and how often they have been rehearsed determine their accessibility.

CONTENT CATEGORIES

We turn now to the content of teachers' memories and the discussion of the findings. Table 2 presents the frequency of

Table 2. Frequency of Content Category References for All Participants

CATEGORY	FREQUENCY	p^a
Focus on students		
References	42	N.S.
Percentage[b]	15.0	
Interpersonal relations		
References	60	< .001
Percentage	21.4	
Rules and principles		
References	46	< .077
Percentage	16.4	
Negative experiences		
References	21	< .001
Percentage	7.5	
Teaching alternatives		
References	31	N.S.
Percentage	11.1	
Situation background		
References	41	N.S.
Percentage	14.6	
Job difficulties		
References	25	< .050
Percentage	8.9	
Positive experiences		
References	14	< .001
Percentage	5.0	
Total references	280	

[a]Proportion of each category compared to mean proportion (.125) using normal approximation to the binomial
[b]Percentage of total references

content category references for all participants as a percentage of the total number of references.

As can be seen, the frequencies of four of these categories were significantly different from chance distribution. The category of interpersonal relations was predominant. Negative experiences, job difficulties, and positive experiences were mentioned significantly less. The category of rules and principles was emphasized by the teachers and approaches significance. Figure 1 displays these results graphically. These results may be interpreted as reflecting the major importance teachers seem to assign to their relationships with others in the context of the workplace. It may well be that teachers' recollections are shaped by their tacit sense of the significance of interpersonal relations. The focus on interpersonal relations in the context of teachers' work contradicts the view that "the cellular form of school organization and the attendant time and space ecology, suits interactions between teachers at the margin of their daily work. Individualism characterizes their socialization; teachers do not share a powerful technical culture" (Lortie 1975, p. 192).

Figure 1. Percentage of each content category references for all participants.

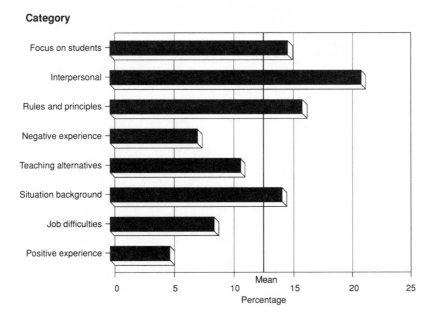

It seems that teachers do tend to view interpersonal relationships as being at the core of their professional experiences. Interpersonal relationships are crucial for the development of a cooperative and sharing school culture, and for the sustained existence of collaborative settings that enable teachers to help each other improve teaching and learning processes in their schools (Rosenholtz 1991).

Another explanation of the predominance of certain content categories concerns distance from the classroom, which can result in "shifts in emphasis and wholesale deletions" (Linton 1986, p. 64). Job difficulties and positive and negative experiences of classroom life recede, and in hindsight the important and meaningful aspects of events are associated with interpersonal relations, on the one hand, and with the essence of professional knowledge in the form of rules and principles, on the other hand.

The following sections discuss the meaning of each of the different content categories and provide some concrete examples of teachers' stories for each category.

Focus on Students

Focus on students is defined as emphasis on the experiences of students, though the main character in the recalled event might still be the teacher. In one of the interviews, Hannah, a participating teacher, said: "I remember events that are related to persons more than events related to materials." The following is an example of focus on students:

> It happened in the '60s. A pair of twin boys were students in parallel eight grades. I taught math in both classes. Once we tried an experimental new math curriculum and conducted a series of model lessons inviting teachers and the superintendent. Each of the twins sat in the first row in his respective class. During the lesson one of the boys became highly involved and enthusiastic and kept interfering, jumping up and down. During the following lesson, in the second class, his twin brother behaved in the same way. At the end of the lesson the superintendent turned to

me and said: "I don't understand, why you brought this unruly child with you from one class to the other."

Event no. 55
Female elementary school teacher
Lower-class population
Years of practice at the time of the event: 17
Overall years of teaching: 30
Years since retirement: 14

This case of humor in the classroom tells about a teacher's experience with a superintendent, but the focus is on the behavior of students. The flavor of this story lies in the teacher's positive retrospective view of her students. We can almost imagine her smile when she shares this recollection with us, though at the time of the event she might have been perturbed by the twins' interruptive behavior.

The following event is another example of focus on students. Not only is this a very vivid and detailed story about a traumatic classroom episode, it is also an example of learning from one's students:

In the break Isri, one of the students, having finished eating, went to the trash basket to throw in some orange peels. He stopped to read some notices which were put on a wall newspaper, supporting himself with his right hand on the classroom door. Another student tried to enter the class, knocked on the door, received permission, and opened the door right on Isri's fingers. The whole matter lasted a couple of seconds. Hearing Isri's cry, the door was reopened, and I took Isri to the nurse's room, where he was treated. We did everything we could to relieve his pain. Without much thinking I scolded the child who had caused injury, though he was very sad and upset. Isri, still very pale and agitated said: "Teacher, it was my fault. He could not have known that I had put my hand at this spot of the door. I should not have done it." I learned several things from this event concerning the following issues:

1. What is the appropriate place for a wall newspaper?
2. How to overcome sudden anger? How to consider the appropriate reaction to students' behavior?
3. How to provide maximum safety in the classroom?
4. A person may be understood not only by his charity, his anger, and his drinking habits (an ancient Hebrew saying), but also by his behavior when in pain. I assume that much more may be learned from the event.

Event no. 7
Female elementary school teacher
Middle-class population
Years of practice at the time of the event: 2
Overall years of teaching: 37
Years since retirement: 12

This is another example of students as heroes. The narrator elaborates on the insights she gained from this event, in the form of rules and principles of practice. The rules may be clear and straightforward, relating to everyday decisions about the placing of students' work or providing safety in the classroom. A general, overriding principle concerns the understanding of students. It is intriguing that the teacher chose to extent the meaning of a well-known ancient Hebrew saying about human nature. Her deep roots in Jewish culture provide a framework for her own new insights into the nature of students. Classrooms can be an arena of much mental pain and psychological stress, inflicted by students and teachers alike. This teacher's story raises the issue of pain in classrooms, stressing the importance of teachers' awareness of students' reactions to painful situations.

Two additional points may be made. The narrator shares her questions with the audience of her story. She does not suggest that she knows how to overcome sudden anger in the classroom, or that she is able to advise others about appropriate reactions to students' behavior. Yet her questions, stemming from a concrete experience, may provide the basis for inquiries into the important issues she raises.

The concluding comment of her story is enlightening: "I assume that much more may be learned from the event." The story is not presented as a closed case of life in classrooms.

The narrator hints that manifold interpretations are possible, that diverse insights may be gained, that she herself, or other teachers, may reach additional pedagogical, or instructional, conclusions. Learning from experience with one's students is portrayed as an open and continuous quest for meaning. Therein lies the beauty of this story.

Interpersonal Relationships

This category reflects teachers' concerns about relationships, whether with their students, their colleagues, principals, superintendents, or parents. The following is an example:

> After three years, in 1972, I was working in Tira. The supervisor there was a very harsh and frightening woman. She used to appear in my dreams like a witch. She admired my work but begrudged me my success. Once she arrived at my kindergarten with a whole group of visitors. I held a tray with apples in my hands. When I saw her, the tray slipped out of my hands and the apples scattered on the floor. Once she screamed at me demanding why I did not have a full list of attendance in my diary. She made me cry. I went to another supervisor in order to resign. I put the keys of the kindergarten on his desk and told him: "I resign." I burst out crying: "I cannot stand this evil supervisor any longer." Sometime later a new supervisor arrived. She was wonderful, supported me greatly, helped me with good advice and warm friendship, thus restoring the supervisor–kindergarten teacher relationship. All-new projects were implemented in my kindergarten. Over many years student-teachers and visitors from abroad used to visit my kindergarten.

Event no. 28
Female kindergarten teacher
Lower-class population
Years of practice at the time of the event: 4
Overall years of teaching: 12
Years since retirement: 10

This episode highlights the fierce emotionality of personal professional relationships and their impact on teachers' perceptions of their environment and their work.

The most meaningful relationships recalled by this teacher concern authority figures in her professional life. Her story emphasizes support, good advice, and warm friendship as crucial features of a positive relationship between supervisors and teachers. A causal link between such positive relationships and successful teaching is implied by the happy ending of the story.

Rules and Principles

Rules are statements that represent the outcomes of teachers' reflections on their experiences and are put in the form of guidance for practice. For instance, Hannah, recalling an event concerning the teaching of grammar, stated that three principles had stayed with her:

1. Every teacher, at every class level, has to view himself or herself as part of a chain.
2. It is very important for all teachers to study the structure of the discipline they teach.
3. Continuous involvement in curriculum development and change is part of the teaching profession. (Assuming that 70 to 80 percent of the curriculum is stable and does not change).

Event no. 6
Female elementary school teacher
Middle-class population
Years of practice at the time of the event: 4
Overall years of teaching: 37
Years since retirement: 12

These rules concern three different facets of teaching, involving the following kinds of views:

- One's view of oneself as member of a community of professionals
- One's view of the knowledge base of teaching
- One's view of the cardinal professional activities of teachers

Retired teachers seem to be quite eager to share their personal rules and principles with the audience of their recollections. Thus, kindergarten teachers voiced the following rules of practice:

One should pay attention to problematic children in kindergarten and ask for psychological assistance. It is wrong to postpone the matter until they go to school. (Event no. 31)

Children who sense that one respects them and treats them fairly will accept everything, even unpleasant decisions. (Event no. 25)

Schoolteachers stated, for instance:

Teachers should visit the homes of problematic children in order to understand the roots of their behavior. (Event no. 57)

Children should be allowed to learn according to their own style and preference. (Event no. 91)

Teachers should be educators and not transmittors of knowledge. (Event no. 58)

These rules express the deep concern for students that characterizes school- and kindergarten teachers who participated in the study. Past experiences are manifest in these brief statements. The "problem" child who needs early attention and assistance, and the different learning styles witnessed by teachers during their years of practice, constitute the background for these declarations.

Elbaz (1983) identifies rules and principles as central components of teachers' practical knowledge. Teachers who, when recalling events from their past professional lives, linked these events to explicit rules and principles, articulated the transformation of experiences into practical, "codified" knowledge. In chapter 8 we'll elaborate this transformation process as perceived by teachers.

Negative Experiences

Negative experiences were more frequent than positive experiences in the recalled events of the retired teachers. An example of such a negative experience is an elementary school teacher's story of an event that took place in her twentieth year of teaching first grade:

> It happened in 1980. One of my students used to spend most of his time outside class. His parents were invited to talk with me. The father hit the mother in front of me. It was awful. I was really shocked. The child told me that his father used to hit him as well. Since then I refrained from reporting on his behavior to the father and dealt only with the mother.

Event no. 119
Female elementary school teacher
Middle-class population
Years of practice at the time of the event: 20
Overall years of teaching: 29
Years since retirement: 1

Teachers may experience upsetting events that because of their unexpectedness and uniqueness tend to be remembered clearly. The event described by this teacher might have been alien to her own childhood experiences and caused her to confront unfamiliar realities and harsh facts. The change in her own behavior seems to have been an attempt to deal with this specific situation, accepting the disclosed pattern of family violence with resignation. It may well be that the teacher perceived home events as being outside her own sphere of competence or authority. In present times teachers might feel more accountable for dealing with such a situation.

Research on memory of events reveals the importance of negative, even traumatic, experiences in one's autobiographical recollections. In Robinson's (1976) study of autobiographical events, 10 percent of reports of past events dealt with injuries and accidents, in spite of a general tendency to favor recall of pleasant or successful experiences. Linton (1986) and Wagenaar (1986) assert that negative memories are rare in their findings.

The relative preponderance of negative experiences in teachers' memories contradicts Linton's (1986) finding that "the content of memory as represented by the recall protocols are curiously silent about specific negative events" (p. 59).

It may be that there is a salient difference between professional memories, which tend to include the negative aspects of past events, and purely personal ones, which might tend to overlook them. The issue might be related to the significance of memory in forming one's sense of self. Kelchterman (1991), in his study of teachers' professional development, found that critical incidents and phases in his respondents' professional biographies served to shape their professional selves and their subjective educational theories. Critical incidents and phases might be judged by the teacher as positive or negative, but it may be assumed that negative experiences are part of the incidents that leave their mark on the professional self.

Teaching Alternatives

The participating teachers were asked to document recalled events of their professional lives. Some of these events, such as alternative teaching modes, were related directly to classroom teaching. Unusual events tend to be recalled more frequently than regular, commonplace ones, as they are beyond the expected frame of a schematized and generalized script (Nelson 1986). Rubin and Kozin (1984) found that clearer memories were surprising, consequential, and emotional. It may be argued that the adaptation, or invention, of teaching alternatives belong to the category of surprising, consequential, and even emotional events. The following event mentioned previously may serve as an example:

> I was a homeroom teacher of the sixth grade. The English teacher was Mr. D., who had previously been my own teacher. True to his approach, he started teaching English grammar as soon as the students began to study English (as a second language) in the fifth grade. When they reached the sixth grade the students were expected to use a fair number of English grammar terms. Mr. D. soon found out that his students were not familiar with the meaning of basic

terms in grammar. He asked us to tell him about the Hebrew grammar curriculum. The principal, two colleagues, and I told him all about it. After a brief discussion we were convinced that students should learn the basic concepts of grammar in their mother tongue before encountering them in another language. We understood that we had to revise our curriculum, paying attention to the inherent differences between the two languages. (Our task would have been easier if the second language had been Arabic.) We consulted with colleagues at the secondary level who were experts in grammar and developed a new curriculum in Hebrew grammar, through which students became acquainted with the basics before the end of the fifth grade. Instruction was based on reading aloud of appropriate texts, leading to comprehension and to familiarity with grammatical rules. Spelling lessons were also devoted to gaining insight into grammar. More than forty years have passed since that time. Many changes have been introduced into the curriculum, but the basic approach of our curriculum was preserved.

Event no. 6
Female elementary school teacher
Middle-class population
Years of practice at the time of the event: 4
Overall years of teaching: 37
Years since retirement: 12

This event demonstrates the nature of professional problems teachers might experience. In this case the problem is not related to issues of devising appropriate modes of explanation of a difficult subject-matter domain, nor does it concern other everyday teaching activities. The story focuses on issues of vertical and horizontal curriculum planning, and on opportunities for integrating different disciplines. The problem was solved through cooperative planning carried out by teachers in consultation with colleagues and experts. The story describes the process of teacher cooperation, illuminating an important aspect of the school ethos. Restructuring the teaching of grammar was an important professional event that left its mark on the school curriculum, as well as on this teacher's autobiographical memory.

Situation Background

Background details might be included in retired teachers' recall of professional events. Background details include statements about the socioeconomic situations of the students, such as their parents' poverty and destitute living quarters. Sometimes the narrator described the physical environment of the school and classroom.

Teachers tended to describe the socioeconomic backgrounds of their students, especially when relating events that took place in the '50s and early '60s, years of massive immigration to Israel. For instance:

> Most inhabitants were new immigrants from Yugoslavia, Yemen, North Africa, and Italy. Most of the children came from poor families. The school provided the main meal of the day.
>
> Event no. 73
> Female elementary school teacher
> Lower-class population
> Years of practice at the time of the event: 4
> Overall years of teaching: 30
> Years since retirement: 7

The time and locality of the reported event was noted in most documented events. This common opening, though part of the background, does not fully characterize the diverse situations and lacks further elaboration of descriptive details. As stated earlier, Rubin and Kozin (1984) claim that clear and vivid memories were more surprising, consequential, and emotional. It may well be the case that more background details were provided by the narrators whenever their memories were indeed more surprising, consequential, or emotional. The following is an example of such an event:

> In my first year of teaching, 1960, in Afula [a small town in the north of Israel], I was assigned a class of

students from very difficult socioeconomic backgrounds. One of the children was Dan. Frequently the children used to complain that the sandwiches they had brought for lunch were missing. They came to me and said: "I don't find my sandwiches." "I don't find my fruit." I had never thought that there would be children in the class who had no food. I was naive, this was my first year of teaching. Each time I thought that the children had forgotten their lunch. Finally we found out that one of the children used to take the sandwiches and eat them while all the other students were at the morning assembly. Each morning the same thing happened. I went to visit the home of this student. He lived in a very poor and shabby neighborhood. His mother opened the door and started immediately to cry and tell me that she had no food for the children and that her husband was unemployed. She overwhelmed me with her woes. I was extremely sad and did not know what to say to her. After some time I introduced myself as her son's teacher. Hearing that, she led me into her home and treated me to coffee and cake. She apologized for crying and for telling me her troubles, and added: "I told you all this because I thought that you are a social worker." It turned out that she used to sleep in the mornings and did not prepare sandwiches for her son.

Event no. 69
Female elementary school teacher
Lower-class population
Years of practice at the time of the event: 1
Overall years of teaching: 28
Years since retirement: 2

There is no doubt that this event left a strong mark on the narrating teacher. It taught her not to be "naive," as she put it, therefore it was highly consequential for her professional attitudes. The event itself was associated with strong emotions, and it had a surprise, unexpected ending. All these factors may have contributed to the vividness of recall and to the elaboration of situational details.

Job Difficulties

Retired teachers mentioned difficulties in their memories. Job difficulties related to perceived obstacles, complications, and pitfalls were part of the experiences teachers reported. These are not necessarily negative experiences; rather, they are instances of grappling with some professional problem. The following event serves as an example:

> In the third year of my work I taught a nongraded elementary class in a camp of new immigrants. The students ranged from age seven to twelve. I tried very hard but lacked the necessary knowledge. All teachers were unusually devoted to their work. We collected one teaspoon of oil and one spoon of flour from each family. I brought a stove from home, we made dough and prepared patties. All the children sat around, and I was in the center, baking the patties. My father, who happened to visit me and saw me in this situation, burst out crying for me.

Event no. 72
Female elementary school teacher
Lower-class population
Years of practice at the time of the event: 3
Overall years of teaching: 30
Years since retirement: 7

A number of difficulties are reflected in this story. The teacher mentions her lack of adequate knowledge in the face of a difficult situation, a nongraded class of new immigrant students. Devotion to one's task is perceived as compensating, at least partially, for the lack of professional knowledge. The most fascinating aspect of this event is the apparently close tie of the teacher with her parents. Her father visited her class and was appalled by the classroom scene. The crying father, whether a reconstruction or an authentic incident, reveals dependence on family involvement, support, and approval, which might be natural for a young woman thrust into a difficult and alien situation. The story raises interesting gender issues concerning the special status and self-image of female teachers in a traditional society.

Do people tend to recall difficulties when they are asked to remember autobiographical events? Kihlstrom (1981) discusses the nature of memory for success and failure experiences, using Gestalt theory as a conceptual framework. This theory leads to the prediction that interrupted or failed tasks would be favored by retention because of the mental activity involved in transforming them to "good form," regularity, completeness, and so on. On the other hand, Kihlstrom states that evidence indicates a general tendency for subjects to recall successful experiences rather than failures. Teachers' recalled events that report failures are partially concerned with unfinished tasks. For instance, in the above-mentioned episode the teacher tells about the difficulties of teaching nongraded classes and states: "I tried very hard, but lacked the necessary knowledge."

Other events that focus on job difficulties might express the expertise of teachers who reflect on their work in retrospect. Some of the difficulties described by teachers were portrayed as the basis for successful problem solving. The following event exemplifies this tendency:

> In the '80s a new school was built in the southern part of K. The population was very heterogenous, new immigrants, old-timers, children from broken homes. I was the homeroom teacher of the fourth grade, with forty-four students. It was very difficult to teach this class because of the large differences between the students. I had to match my teaching to different levels of knowledge. I used to prepare varied plans and learning activities, and different worksheets. The better students assisted the weaker ones. We taught many hours and stayed overtime to help the weak students with their homework. These additional teaching hours helped the weaker students and improved their achievements.

> Event no. 51
> Female elementary school teacher
> Heterogeneous population
> Years of practice at the time of the event: 21
> Overall years of teaching: 35
> Years since retirement: 1

This teacher had planned varied instructional strategies in order to cope with the extreme socioeconomic heterogeneity of her students. The tone of the event is positive, in spite of the grave difficulties mentioned in the story. Again teachers' devotion and commitment is conceived of as the way to deal with these difficulties, and the positive results were taken as justifying these special efforts.

Positive Experiences

The "Pollyanna principle" has been demonstrated by Matlin and Stang (1978) to be a powerful agent in cognition and memory. According to this principle, people tend to recall positive and successful experiences. Wagenaar (1986) showed that pleasant events were better recalled than neutral or unpleasant ones. One possible explanation is that pleasant events are more salient to the narrator. In Wagenaar's study of his own recall of 2,400 events from his daily life, very pleasant and very unpleasant events behaved symmetrically with respect to emotional involvement. According to Wagenaar, memories of unpleasant events are suppressed in congruence with Freudian theory. Still, Wagenaar concludes that the experimental literature concerning the effects of pleasantness on memory is not very conclusive.

Woods (1987) argues that teachers' memories permit "a celebration of self and enhancement of the primary rewards of teaching" (p. 128). This celebration of self may account for those memories that focus on positive experiences.

According to Linton (1986), contents of memory reflect a "generally integrated, cheerful view of a life" (p. 60). In their later life period, after retirement, teachers may tend to recall events that present such an integrated, positive view of life, as expressed in the following example:

> I organized a performance in the second grade. This happened eight years ago. The theme was "My country." I wrote the text with the children. Many songs, stories, proverbs, landscapes were part of the performance. We sang and danced. The performance was so moving and successful that we repeated it at the

end-of-term ceremony for graduates. It gave us a wonderful feeling.

> Event no. 115
> Female elementary school teacher
> Middle-class population
> Years of practice at the time of the event: 21
> Overall years of teaching: 29
> Years since retirement: 1

This is a glowing report of an event in which different aspects of teaching come together to create a "moving and successful performance." The teacher wrote the text herself, relying on her talent and inventiveness. The performance itself integrated diverse components, and, last but not least, it was received so well by the audience that it was chosen to be repeated at the school graduation ceremony. The whole story reflects a highly positive view of teaching.

We have discussed the content of teachers' recollections, trying to understand the possible meaning of their varied stories. We have seen that some principles of memory of events seem to apply to the recalling of professional events. Unexpected or unique occurrences, events that were perceived as consequential for teachers' lives, as well as traumatic experiences, were reflected in the content of teachers' stories. On the other hand, their recollections were not silent concerning negative incidents; such silence is a feature of memory of events, according to Linton (1986). Teachers' stories include unforgotten negative experiences, though many of the recalled events reflect the positive aspects of practice. This tendency of teachers to look back with satisfaction on their professional lives will be discussed in chapter 5.

TEXT QUANTITY

To determine the overall emphasis teachers assigned to the various content categories, text quantity was correlated with the eight content categories by means of a Pearson correlation. More text was associated with focus on students ($r = .23$, $p < .01$), with rules and principles ($r = .30$, $p < .001$), with teaching alternatives ($r = .23$, $p < .01$), and with job difficulties ($r = .26$, $p < .01$). All these categories are closely linked to the nature of teaching. The larger number of words used by teachers to describe these themes, even though the theme itself might not be very common in the overall analysis of events, reflects their focus on the professional aspects of recalled events.

BACKGROUND VARIABLES OF TEACHERS

The only significant correlation between content categories and the background variables of teachers was a negative correlation between years of practice at the time of the recalled event and the "situation background" category. Teachers who had more years of practice at the time of the reported event tended to provide fewer background descriptions ($r = .36$, $p < .001$). This phenomenon may be interpreted as reflecting Linton's (1982) finding that events that contain familiar elements and configurations are more difficult to distinguish from singular events. Linton claims that "in representations of personal events a number of basic semantic elements are repeatedly used and eventually configurations of these basic elements are themselves repeated, making it difficult to provide unique event descriptions" (p. 86). As background details became part of a generalized configuration of the past, retired teachers may find it more difficult, and maybe even unnecessary, to provide specific descriptions of background situations of the recalled events.

SUMMARY COMMENTS

Analysis of teachers' stories yielded eight different content categories: focus on students, interpersonal relations, rules and principles, negative experiences, teaching alternatives, situation background, job difficulties, and positive experiences.

The "interpersonal relations" category was predominant in teachers' memories, apparently being at the core of their professional experiences. The different content categories were discussed, and concrete examples of teachers' stories for each category were provided. Some principles of memory of events seem to apply to the recalling of professional events by retired teachers. Unexpected or unique occurrences, events that were perceived as consequential for teachers' lives, as well as traumatic experiences, were reflected in the content of teachers' stories. Many of the recalled events reflect the positive aspects of practice, though numerous events focus on negative experiences.

3

The Impact of Teaching Situations
on Teachers' Memories

The relevant sociocultural context of curriculum consists of those extra-systemic demographic, social, political, and economic conditions, traditions and
ideologies, and events that influence curriculum and
curriculum change.

Cornbleth 1990, p. 31

🌱 ONE of the main issues in our study concerns the nature
of the impact of different teaching situations on teachers' memories. In which ways does the context determine the content of
teachers' memories? The first set of findings relates to differences between memories of kindergarten teachers and memories of schoolteachers.

MEMORIES OF KINDERGARTEN TEACHERS AND
SCHOOLTEACHERS: WHAT IS THE DIFFERENCE?

Kindergarten teachers and schoolteachers work in very different educational environments. The Israeli kindergarten is usually located in special buildings that are not connected to a
school. Generally two to four kindergarten teachers are responsible for one or two classes, without a principal. Many kinder-
gartens have an abundance of resources, a play yard, toys, and
instructional materials. The educational focus is on personal
and social development, combined with the acquisition of learning skills and some basic school-oriented knowledge in math,
science, art, and such. Much emphasis is put on interpersonal
development and on the creation of a culturally meaningful
environment. The educational philosophy is child oriented rather

45

than subject-matter oriented. Achievement testing is generally abhorred, though lately there is a growing tendency to view the kindergarten as a preparatory stage for school, enhancing the importance of "academic" activities, such as carrying out experiments and using worksheets. Schools, even those that serve grades 1 through 6, are driven by an academic achievement philosophy, with more and more attention being given to a subject-matter specialization. It is not unusual to find five or more teachers teaching one elementary class. Besides the homeroom teacher, who teaches reading, Bible studies, and some form of social studies, there might be separate teachers for math, science, art, English, and physical education. The number of students in one elementary school may be about two hundred to four hundred, with twenty to thirty teachers, a principal, and some administrative staff. The result is a bustling and lively workplace, with a busy teachers' lounge and much teacher interaction.

Does this environmental difference express itself in the themes reflected in the recalled events of retired teachers? Table 3 presents frequencies of references for each of the eight content categories by the two types of teachers. The relation between content category and type of teacher was examined separately for each of the eight categories. As can be seen in table 3, no significant relations emerged. The apparent homogeneity in themes of recollected events might be due to the general nature of the content categories, which did not provide the basis for more-subtle distinctions between teacher types. To overcome this limitation, references of subcategories of the "rules and principles" category were computed by type of teachers. The subcategories were these: relating to students, relating to parents, relating to teaching alternatives, relating to teachers.

Table 4 shows frequencies for the four subcategories by the two types of teachers. Because teachers did not contribute to more than one category, all categories were analyzed together. Chi-square proved significant (χ^2 [1] = 8.68, $p < .05$). Examination of the residuals within the table indicated that the significant result was due to substantial departure from expectation in the student and teacher subcategories. Figure 2 displays these results graphically.

As can be seen in table 4 and figure 2, kindergarten teachers and schoolteachers show significant differences in their

Table 3. Frequency of Content Category References by Type of Teacher

| | TYPE OF TEACHER | | |
Category	School	Kindergarten	p^a
Focus on students			
References	29	13	N.S.
Percentage[b]	16.0	13.0	
Interpersonal relations			
References	36	24	N.S.
Percentage	20.0	24.0	
Rules and principles			
References	30	16	N.S.
Percentage	16.7	16.0	
Negative experiences			
References	14	7	N.S.
Percentage	7.8	7.0	
Teaching alternatives			
References	20	11	N.S.
Percentage	11.0	11.0	
Situation background			
References	23	18	N.S.
Percentage	12.8	18.0	
Job difficulties			
References	18	7	N.S.
Percentage	10.0	7.0	
Positive experiences			
References	10	4	N.S.
Percentage	5.6	4.0	
Total references	180	100	

[a]Evaluated using chi-square
[b]Percentage of total references

emphasis on rules and principles relating to students or to their fellow teachers.

Examples of teacher rules and principles were presented above. Let us examine some more. A kindergarten teacher said: "One thinks that small children don't understand, but when one explains well, they understand everything" (Event no. 26). Or "When children come willingly to kindergarten, it is possible

Table 4. Frequency of Rule and Principle Subcategory References by Type of Teacher

	TYPE OF TEACHER	
Subcategory	School	Kindergarten
Relating to students		
References	10	11
Percentage[a]	33.3	69.0
Relating to parents		
References	3	3
Percentage	10.0	19.0
Relating to teaching alternatives		
References	4	1
Percentage	13.3	6.0
Relating to teachers		
References	13	1
Percentage	43.3	6.0
Total references	30	16

Note. Chi-square for complete table significant at $p < .05$.
[a]Percentage of total references

Figure 2. Percentage of rule and principle subcategory references by type of teacher. Only categories for which there were large differences (based on chi-square residuals) are displayed.

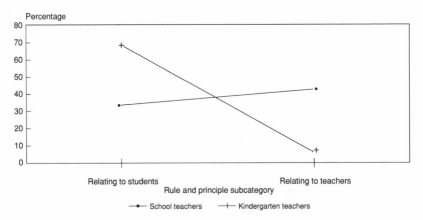

to teach them. Therefore it is important to create a warm and friendly atmosphere in kindergarten" (Event no. 41). The emphasis is on understanding the special needs of small children.

Schoolteachers defining rules and principles concerning their colleagues made statements like these:

> Cooperation and mutual assistance are important principles for successful teaching. (Event no. 76)

> One has to limit bureaucratic procedures such as term reports, so that teachers can be free to be 'educators.' (Event no. 83)

The focus is on teachers, their character, and their mode of working with others.

It seems that kindergarten teachers, whose professional demands were more student-centered than subject-matter oriented, had internalized this approach, and reflected it in their memories. Kindergarten teachers are more accountable for the physical and emotional well-being of their students than for their academic achievement. This commitment determines to a large extent their generic personal memories, the generic images of their experiences (Brewer 1986). When expressing their rules and principles, kindergarten teachers focus mainly on students, while schoolteachers, who also voice rules concerning students, tended to be somewhat more involved in stating rules and principles about interacting with colleagues.

Table 5 presents subcategories of the "interpersonal relations" category, computed by types of teacher. The subcategories are teacher–superiors, teacher–colleagues, teacher–parents, and teacher–students.

Chi-square proved significant for the complete table ($\chi^2[1] = 16.5$, $p < .001$). Examination of the residuals within the table indicated that the significant result was due to substantial departure from expectation in the "teacher–superiors" and "teacher–parents" subcategories. Figure 3 displays these results graphically.

The context of the different teaching situations explains the tendency of schoolteachers to recollect more instances of interpersonal relations with their superiors than kindergarten teachers do, who only rarely interact with superiors. Conversely,

Table 5. Frequency of Interpersonal Relations Subcategory References by Type of Teacher

	TYPE OF TEACHER	
Subcategory	School	Kindergarten
Teacher–superiors		
References	14	1
Percentage[a]	38.9	4.2
Teacher–colleagues		
References	3	2
Percentage	8.3	8.3
Teacher-parents		
References	9	18
Percentage	25.0	75.0
Teacher-students		
References	10	3
Percentage	27.8	12.5
Total references	36	24

Note. Chi-square for complete table significant at $p < .001$.
[a]Percentage of total references

Figure 3. Percentage of interpersonal relations subcategory references by type of teacher. Only categories for which there were large differences (based on chi-square residuals) are displayed.

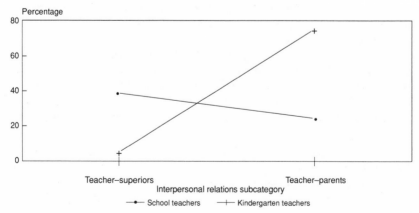

kindergarten teachers are in daily intimate interaction with the parents of kindergarten students, while schoolteachers have fewer opportunities for such contacts.

The professional memories of teachers seem to include ideological and theoretical constructs. Vividness of recall is sometimes ascribed to personal and/or general importance (Rubin and Kozin 1984; Brown and Kulik 1977). Personal and general importance of teachers' memories tends to encompass the teachers' educational philosophy and their specific work context, as demonstrated by the different emphasis on certain themes in events reported by kindergarten teachers versus schoolteachers, in the "rules and principles" and "interpersonal relations" categories.

EVENT PERIOD AND ITS IMPACT ON THEMES OF MEMORY

The recalled professional events related to different historical periods. About half of all recalled events occurred in the first years of practice. In many cases the first years of teaching were historically and socially significant—years of milestone events in the life of Israel. The establishment of the State of Israel, and the large-scale immigration of Holocaust survivors, on one hand, and of refugees from North African and Asian countries, on the other hand, created many difficulties. The population of Israel doubled, and the educational system had to be expanded accordingly. Moreover, most immigrants came with little or no property and lacked knowledge about the country, its language, and its culture. These circumstances were remembered by the teachers as having a profound impact on their professional experiences, and shaped the nature of their memories of that period.

To determine the impact of the historical context on the content of recalled events, these were categorized according to the following timeline:

1. Years of massive immigration—immediately after the establishment of the State of Israel in 1948, up to 1953
2. Years before and immediately after the Six-Day War, from 1954 to 1970
3. The time after the Six-Day War from 1971 to 1990

Of the 135 recorded events, 124 (92%) were dated by the narrators. Of 280 references, therefore, 258 (92%) could be dated. Altogether 25 events (20% of all dated events) were categorized as years of massive immigration. Forty-nine events (40%) occurred before or soon after the Six-Day War, and 50 events (40%) were more recent. Table 6 presents frequency of content-category references by event period. As can be seen,

Table 6. Frequency of Content Category References by Event Period

Category	Immigration	Pre-Six-Day-War	Post-Six-Day-War	p^a
		EVENT PERIOD		
Focus on students				
References	5	16	17	N.S.
Percentage[b]	10	14	17	
Interpersonal relations				
References	7	26	22	N.S.
Percentage	15	23	22	
Rules and principles				
References	5	12	25	< .005
Percentage	10	11	25	
Negative experiences				
References	2	9	10	N.S.
Percentage	4	8	10	
Teaching alternatives				
References	7	9	11	N.S.
Percentage	15	8	11	
Situation background				
References	14	21	4	< .001
Percentage	29	19	4	
Job difficulties				
References	8	14	1	< .001
Percentage	17	13	1	
Positive experiences				
References	—	4	9	< .050
Percentage	0	4	9	
Total references	48	111	99	

[a]Evaluated using chi-square
[b]Percentage of total references

there was a significant relationship between event period and content category for four of the eight categories. Figure 4 displays the categories in which significant results emerged.

Table 6 shows that rules and principles are noted significantly more in teachers' memories of the period after the Six-Day War. At this time in their teaching career there seemed to occur a consolidation of professional knowledge, which was communicated by the narrators to their immediate audience. This process of consolidation might be strengthened by the tendency of elderly people to resolve past experiences. Conway (1990) states that "life review, reworking and reevaluation of memories, and generally resolving past experiences, appear to be a feature of autobiographical memory in the elderly" (p. 154).

As can be seen from table 6, significantly more situation background was mentioned in events occurring during the immigration years. This finding is consistent with other research on memory of events (Rubin and Kozin 1984). Importance of event features at the time the event happened, as well as the novelty of the experiences, appears to determine the clarity of recalled events. The impact of historical contexts does not express itself solely in number of references that mention the situation background. The nature of background details changes over time, as reflected in the comparison of two events:

Figure 4. Percentage of content category references by event period. Only categories for which there were significant differences are displayed.

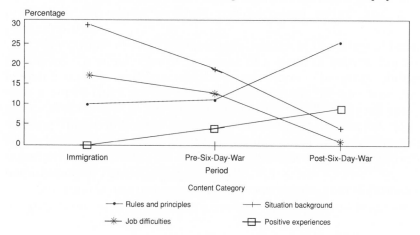

In the year 1951 I worked in Mishmar Hayam, a community of new immigrants. Each family had received a number of rooms in a large cabin according to the number of family members. There were Poles, Romanians, and people from Czechoslovakia. I did not know their languages, and they did not know Hebrew. I learned Yiddish from them. I remember that at the beginning I felt completely lost. When a child wept I could not understand him. The Ministry of Education obliged me to live there. I had no one to talk with in the evenings. Sometimes I went home. There was a shortage of toys and materials. I worked there for four years. There were some disabled children in the kindergarten. The parents were Holocaust survivors with many problems. I tried to encourage the parents to participate in festivities and birthdays. Slowly, they learned Hebrew. After six months the children helped me to communicate with their parents. My main task was to teach them Hebrew, basic skills, and responsibilities. The children were quite spoiled by their parents. When I meet my former students today, we kiss and talk about the past. They are glad to see me. They remind me of my former haircut. They are very happy to meet me and invite me to their family gatherings. Our relations are wonderful.

Event no. 1
Female kindergarten teacher
Lower-class population
Years of practice at the time of the event: 1
Overall years of teaching: 36
Years since retirement: 5

In 1974 I worked in Habonim kindergarten. The population was well established. The starting point of my work was very high. Teaching strategies had changed and were adapted to the individual needs of children. We had learned a lot ourselves through inservice programs. We worked closely with the parents, especially in field trips and all kinds of festivities. All children ate lunch at the kindergarten, we were not allowed to send them home for lunch. I remember that one mother wrote to the Ministry of Education to be exempted from the common lunch.

Event no. 46
Female kindergarten teacher
Middle-class population
Years of practice at the time of the event: 20
Overall years of teaching: 32
Years since retirement: 5

Major differences in the situations described by these two kindergarten teachers are noticeable. In the '50s, teachers may have felt completely alienated, lacking a means of communicating with children and parents, working without basic resources. Twenty years later the tone of the recollected event has changed. One discerns a sense of satisfaction with the situation. The nature of perceived and recollected difficulties has changed, and latter-day difficulties seem almost trivial, compared to those experienced in earlier years.

The farther back in time recollections go, the more they emphasize job difficulties, reflecting the impact of contextual factors on teachers' memories of events. The "good old times" were difficult, as can be seen in the events presented above.

Positive experiences were significantly more abundant in the memories of the period after the Six-Day War. These were years of greater personal professional confidence and certainty, possibly related to the development of pedagogical expertise. The events recorded for this period occurred before the "awakening" of Israelis to the harsh fact of the ongoing political and economic crisis. This accounts for the general sense of satisfaction, pervading teachers' memories of this period, in their professional lives. Moreover, it may well be that the Pollyanna principle is stronger in "field memories"—cases in which the memory maintains the perspective the rememberer had at the time of the experience. Nigro and Neisser (1983) observed that field memories were more frequent for recent events. As demonstrated earlier, as recent events tend to be more positive from the point of view of retired teachers, their recollections of these events are richer in positive experiences.

THE IMPACT OF THE NATURE OF
STUDENT POPULATIONS ON TEACHERS'
PROFESSIONAL MEMORIES

We have seen that the teaching context influences to some extent the nature of teachers' memories. What impact do specific kinds of student populations have on teachers' professional memories? Table 7 presents the frequency of content-

Table 7.   Frequency of Content Category References by Type of Student Population

Category	TYPE OF STUDENT POPULATION (CLASSES)			
	Lower-class	Middle-class	Heterogeneous	p^a
Focus on students				
References	9	22	11	N.S.
Percentage[b]	14	19	11	
Interpersonal relations				
References	12	28	20	N.S.
Percentage	18	24	20	
Rules and principles				
References	4	19	23	< .050
Percentage	6	16	24	
Negative experiences				
References	8	7	6	N.S.
Percentage	12	6	6	
Teaching alternatives				
References	2	19	10	< .050
Percentage	3	16	10	
Situation background				
References	21	6	14	< .001
Percentage	32	5	14	
Job difficulties				
References	7	7	11	N.S.
Percentage	11	6	11	
Positive experiences				
References	3	8	3	N.S.
Percentage	5	7	3	
Total references	66	116	98	

[a]Evaluated using chi-square
[b]Percentage of total references

category references by type of student population. Student populations were categorized as follows: lower-class, middle-class, and heterogeneous.

As in the case of event period, each content category was analyzed separately. Three significant associations emerged. These are displayed in figure 5.

Several content categories of memories are significantly different when reported in relation to lower-class versus middle-class or heterogeneous populations. The category of rules and principles looms larger in the events concerning heterogeneous classes than in those related to middle-class or lower-class populations. Teachers might have found the heterogeneous context more demanding and more challenging, and so they might have formed more generalized guides for action based on their experiences in such classes. Teachers might also have wished to share with others their hard-won insights about heterogeneous classes.

Teaching alternatives is a content area that appears significantly more often in the memories of teachers who taught middle-class and heterogeneous classes than in the memories of teachers of students who came from a lower-class socioeconomic milieu. This finding may be understood to reflect teachers' aspirations to create manifold learning opportunities for

Figure 5. Percentage of content category references by student population. Only categories for which there were significant differences are displayed.

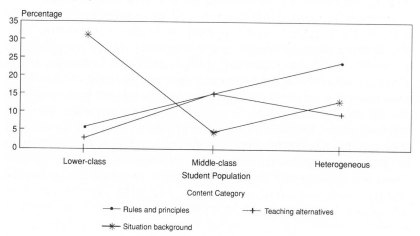

"better" and more motivated students. This aspiration may be contrary to a common approach of teachers in working-class schools, who often use restricted procedures and simple instructional tasks such as copying notes and answering textbooks questions (Anyon 1981). The limited teaching alternatives that characterize the curriculum in use in working-class schools, according to Anyon, might be legitimated by teachers on the grounds that other instructional strategies might be too difficult for the students. More elaborated and sophisticated instructional needs might be conceived as "useless" for working-class students. One of the teachers in Anyon's study is quoted as saying: "I don't do the tests [provided by the science textbook]. It's too depressing. They never get it and they'll never *use* it" (p. 10, emphasis in the original).

The high number of references to teaching alternatives provided by teachers of heterogeneous classes may reflect their attempts to respond to the perceived needs of different students, who could not be expected to benefit from one set of instructional practices.

Most significant were the differences concerning the content category "situation background," which characterized the recalled events of teachers of lower-class students. Several reasons might account for this phenomenon. It might be that the teachers, who came from a middle-class background, found the background of their students so strange and unexpected, and so far removed from their own life experiences, that these circumstances had the characteristics of events that are well recalled. Thus, uniqueness and unexpectedness not only are features of well-remembered whole events (Linton 1979; Rubin and Kozin 1984), but they might function also as determinants of recall of components of recorded events.

Another explanation of the richness of background details incorporated in the events recorded by teachers of working-class students may be that this is a narrative artifact introduced by the narrator in the process of constructing the remembered story. Neisser (1986) argued that recall was almost always constructive. According to Neisser, the largest amount of elaboration takes place when one offers an account to another person. The reporting teachers may have perceived the need for elaboration because of the large gap in time, and in conditions, between the educational situation in which they used to practice and the present-day context of schooling.

The findings of this study have shown some commonality of memory content for all teachers, as well as some distinctive differences between memories of teachers in varying situations. One may view these findings as pertaining to the "collective professional memory" of teachers working in specific contexts. Collective memory (Halbwachs 1980) constitutes the shared meanings of a community. Bellah and colleagues (1985) speak of communities of memory that do not forget their past. Carrying a context of shared meaning, they turn toward the future. Being part of such communities of memory is deemed highly important for professionals. The study of teachers' memories indicated that teachers may be perceived as sharing collective memories. The process of development of individual and collective memories is discussed in chapter 8.

TENURE CHARACTERISTICS AND THE AFFECTIVE QUALITY OF TEACHERS' MEMORIES

The affective quality of memory has interested many researchers of memory. Conway (1990), summing up some of this research, states that "increased emotional intensity and life impact are, in fact, important determinants of memory clarity and availability" (p. 92). Conway cites the work of Pillemer and colleagues (1988), who found that the best predictors of clarity of memory were emotional intensity and perceived life impact at the time of experience. Wagenaar (1986) suggested that "salient and emotionally involving events have longer lasting ripples" (p. 239). Wagenaar's study showed that pleasant events were better recalled than unpleasant ones were. He concluded that "the observation regarding unpleasant events suggests that their memories really are suppressed, just as Freud told us" (p. 240). Wagenaar found the difference between the retrieval of pleasant events and the retrieval of unpleasant events to be largest for recent events. It looks as if unpleasant memories lose their sting over time—they are forgotten together with the pleasant memories.

Retired teachers tended to mention negative experiences more often than positive experiences (see table 2). In both cases the level of emotionality and personal significance was high. This common characteristic of teachers' memories is ascribed to the unique demands of professional life. Learning from one's negative experiences is crucial for teachers. Moreover, the narrating teachers might be motived to share stories that reflect past hardships and their own ability to overcome severe difficulties. It is important to note that recalling professional events for a, presumably, professional audience may impose certain constraints on the process of retrieval, and on the content of teachers' stories.

In the search for the effect of recency on the nature of remembered events, the relationship between tenure characteristics and the affective quality of teachers' memories was examined. Table 8 displays tenure characteristics by positive and nonpositive teacher memories. The tenure characteristics were memory recency, years of practice at the time of the recalled event, and years since retirement.

For all three variables, significant results emerged. Thus, teachers whose memories are more positive tended to have worked longer at their profession, recalled more recent memories, and had retired more recently. Figure 6 displays these results graphically.

Retired teachers tended to report significantly more positive memories, the more recent the events were and the closer they were to retirement. The effect of years of practice at the time of the recalled event on its affective tone may be explained

Table 8. Relationships between Tenure Characteristics and Affective Quality of Memory

	AFFECTIVE QUALITY			
Tenure Characteristic	Positive		Nonpositive	
	Mean[a]	Sd	Mean	Sd
Memory recency	16.5	10.1	25.0	12.0
Years on the job	18.9	10.4	12.3	9.8
Years since retirement	3.6	2.7	5.9	4.1

Note: All differences significant at $p < .05$ (evaluated using unpaired *t*-tests).

[a]All means expressed in years.

Figure 6. Affective quality of memory by tenure characteristics. All positive/nonpositive differences were significant.

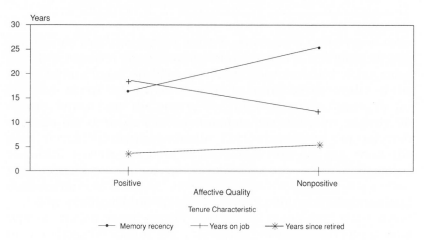

as reflecting the changed context of the teachers' teaching practice, on one hand, and their greater expertise in handling difficulties, on the other hand.

TEACHERS' VIEWS ABOUT RECALL

What keeps memories of events alive? Why do some memories survive and thrive over time? When the teachers in this study were asked about the survival of their memories, these are the sorts of things they mentioned as being most likely to stay in memory:

- Unusual or surprising incidents that leave their mark on teachers' practice
- Enjoyable events
- Sad or traumatic events
- Events that caused great anger or frustration
- Unsuccessful experiences
- Events in which people play a major role
- Dilemma situations concerning teaching

Most of these involve emotions.

Several common factors can be identified among the kinds of events cited as being most likely to be remembered. One is the level of emotions connected with the past experience. Out of fifteen teachers, thirteen mentioned a high level of affect as determining the recall of professional events. The level of surprise of past events was rated as very important by nine of the teachers. Personal importance was considered by ten teachers as affecting retention and recall of events. The teachers' views concerning survival of memories are very close to the findings of researchers. Conway (1990) sums up these findings by stating that they suggest that "the emotional intensity and personal significance of an event give rise to autobiographical memories which are detailed, highly available for recall, and comparatively resistant to forgetting" (p. 104).

SUMMARY COMMENTS

The impact of various factors on the nature of recalled events was examined and discussed in this chapter. These factors are school level (kindergarten teachers or schoolteachers), event period, and the socioeconomic level of the student population. Several content categories of memories were found to be significantly different in varied contexts. The notion of "collective memory" was introduced to account for some commonalities and situation-specific differences in the content of teachers' recalled events. The affective quality of teachers' memories was examined in relation to tenure characteristics of the participating teachers. Teachers whose memories were more positive tended to have worked longer at their profession, recalled more recent memories, and had retired more recently. This effect may be explained as reflecting the changing context of their teaching practice, and their greater expertise at handling difficulties. Teachers' views about factors determining retrieval were reviewed. Most of the factors mentioned by teachers involved the professional and emotional significance of the event at the time of its occurrence.

4

Scripts in Teachers' Memories

Those who don't study the past will repeat its errors.
Those who do study it, will find other ways to err.
Wolf's Law (Dickson 1978, p. 186–87)

🌿 A main question posed in this book is how the process of abstraction and generalization from experience works for teachers who learn from their experiences and construct their professional knowledge.

One of the ways in which past experience is transformed into guides for action is through the development of "scripts"—recipes for understanding situations and acting in them. In chapter 1, scripts were discussed as representing generic personal memories. The present chapter elaborates the notion of scripts and discusses the professional scripts of retired teachers.

THE NATURE OF SCRIPTS

Scripts can be defined as "sequences of actions which are temporally and causally ordered and which are goal directed" (Cohen 1989, p. 110). Schank and Abelson suggested in 1977 that people develop schemas, or scripts, that represent commonly experienced events, such as going to a restaurant. These scripts represent a generalization of past experiences and serve as guides for understanding further experiences, and as a basis for appropriate action. Examples of commonly experienced events for teachers are teaching a lesson, meeting with parents, and having a break in the teachers' lounge. What can we learn from teachers' memories concerning the formation of scripts and their role in teachers' practice? First, let us turn to the notion of a script and its meaning in learning from experience. Schank

(1982) states that "we want to understand how the human mind processes experiences. We want to know how it copes with new information and derives new knowledge from that information. To do all this we need a coherent theory of adaptable memory structures—in other words, a dynamic memory" (p. 4).

In their earlier work Schank and Abelson (1977) considered scripts to be structures that describe sequences of events in particular contexts. Scripts are supposed to be useful sources of predictions of events and appropriate behaviors. The development of scripts is tied to the repetition of experiences in specific situations. In Schank's (1982) words, "The usual method of acquisition of script-based information is direct repeated experience, but people acquire general information in a more complex fashion—by abstracting and generalizing from multiple experiences and from the experiences of others" (p. 9).

Therefore Schank suggested a more dynamic model of memory, considering scripts and other memory structures as capable of self-modification. Generalized scripts are examples of such structures (e.g., the general structure for car driving). According to Schank this modification is based on mismatches between a generalized structure and an experienced event. "If an item is matched by a general structure, it is understood as being of no use to remember. On the other hand, when an experienced event differs from the general structure, its difference may be noted. Noticing and recalling differences of the same kind enables learning. We modify our old structures on the basis of mismatches. This is what a dynamic memory is all about" (Schank 1982, p. 14).

Examples of such deviations are offered by Schank in the context of a restaurant script, which commonly consists of the following sequence: entering, seating, ordering, eating, paying, and leaving. As soon as an "unusual" event, such as walking out of the restaurant without paying, occurs, normal processing of information stops, and the new episode is stored in mind as an entire scene that can be recalled in the future. Scenes are, according to Schank, structures of memory that provide a physical setting that serves as a basis for reconstruction. Schank gives hotel rooms as examples of scenes that can be part of manifold structures, such as the trip structure, the visit structure, and the business deal structure. "The role of a script attached to a scene is to color the scene with the particulars of that scene. In other words, a script is a copy of a scene with particulars filled in. For a script to be used, a copy of the scene is made that alters the scene in appropriate ways, leaving intact the parts of the scene that fit perfectly" (Schank 1982, p. 139).

The notion of scenes as physical settings of memory structures seems highly relevant for gaining insights into teachers' professional memories. Teachers moving from one classroom setting to another can be conceived as comparing and matching scenes of experienced classrooms—leaving intact the parts that fit the scene of their original script, while adapting and changing their script in response to the new experience.

Limited memory structures, such as scripts, can be connected, according to Schank, by more-generalized structures, termed "memory organization packets" (MOPs). A teacher may have acquired a memory organization packet (MOP) concerning "conversations with mothers" that might relate to different scripts, such as "visiting a student's home" or "inviting parents to school." The event of a mother's bursting unexpectedly into a classroom may be processed as being part of the "conversations with mothers" MOP or a "disturbances in classroom" MOP. MOPs contain information that cover many settings, whereas scripts are limited to sequences of actions in one setting. Thus, one can learn across contexts. This conception of memory provides insights into the growth of professional knowledge—when teachers, for instance, might integrate experiences related to students from many scripts and scenes in the classroom, the playground, and the home settings.

Research on scripts was carried out by several investigators of event memory. Bower, Black, and Turner (1979) asked students to make lists of actions that comprise certain events, such as attending a lecture, in the order of their occurrence. They found that there was a substantial agreement about the component actions and their temporal sequence. The findings of their study confirm the psychological reality of scripts.

WHAT ABOUT TEACHERS' SCRIPTS?

"Memory for personal experiences has other functions besides that of reinforcing personal identity. It provides us with a store of 'recipes' for handling current problems and current situations" (Cohen 1989, p. 109). What is the nature of teachers' scripts for recurrent situations, such as managing a lesson? Fifteen retired teachers were asked to provide a list of components of a typical lesson in their regular sequence, Table 9 presents the common elements in these scripts.

In spite of the common elements that constitute the basis of a lesson script, as conceived by the teachers, there are many idiosyncratic details that several respondents included in their scripts. The common elements were these: opening routines, checking for homework, presentation of a new topic, elaboration of the new topic (discussion), summing up, and assigning homework. There is substantial agreement concerning these components of a lesson script and their temporal sequence. These common elements are not very different from those advocated by Herbart, a German education scholar. Herbart (1850–52) suggested several formal stages of a lesson that aim at engaging the minds of students so that they can reach ever-higher levels of knowledge and understanding. According to Herbart a lesson plan should include opportunities for presentation of new matter and ideas, for linking these new components with previously existing knowledge, for elaboration and discussion, and, finally, for practicing and relearning. The commonality of basic components in the practice of teachers suggests that there may exist a shared culture of teaching across time and place.

Teacher scripts exemplify the definition of scripts as goal-directed sequences of actions which are temporally and causally ordered. The inner logic of the scripted sequence of teacher actions in a lesson is clear. Teachers tend to proceed from dealing with established knowledge to introduction of new topics. The lesson tends to start and conclude with homework, thus connecting learning in different, equally important, sites— classroom and home. At the beginning of the lesson, students are requested to report on their home learning; at the end of the lesson the circle closes, and learning is again carried from school to home. Homework not only provides a link between learning inside and outside of school, it also ties new knowledge to prior knowledge. This cycle is very powerful and clearly goal-directed: to maintain a climate of study that is devoted to a body of knowledge to be mastered by the students. The lesson script is analogous to activity structures as described and analyzed by Leinhardt, Weidman, and Hammond (1987): "Activ-

Table 9. Common Elements of Lesson Scripts (in sequence)

ACTIVITIES / No. of script	CHECKING ATTENDANCE	CHECKING HOMEWORK	PRESENTATION OF NEW TOPIC	DISCUSSION (ELABORATION OF NEW TOPIC)	SUMMING UP	ASSIGNING HOMEWORK
1		•	•	•	•	•
2	•	•	•	•	•	•
3		•	•	•	•	•
4			•	•		•
5			•	•	•	•
6	•	•	•	•	•	•
7	•	•	•	•		•
8	•	•	•	•	•	•
9	•	•	•	•		
10	•		•	•	•	•
11		•	•	•	•	•
12			•	•		•
13			•	•	•	•
14			•	•	•	•
15	•		•	•	•	•
Total	7	8	15	15	11	14

ity structures are goal directed segments of teacher and student behavior that involve teachers and students in particular actions, for example, lesson presentation or boardwork" (p. 135). The various components of teachers' scripts discussed above represent such activity structures. According to Leinhardt and colleagues, activity structures are supported by teachers' routines, which are "shared socially scripted patterns of behavior" that "serve to reduce the cognitive complexity of the instructional environment" (p. 135). Leinhardt and Greeno (1986) propose that "routines and activity segments constrain some of the task elements by making them more or less static and transform some of the tasks into highly standard elements that call up entire repertoires of mutually understood behaviors" (p. 94).

"Entire repertoires of mutually understood behaviors" may be perceived as being close to the "memory organization packets" suggested by Schank (1982). The overall typical organization lesson may be understood as representing a generalized structure covering many classroom settings. Yet, as Schank (1982) argues, "the role of a MOP is to provide a place to store new inputs" (p. 83). We shall see how teachers modify this generalized structure.

It is interesting to note that whereas Schank (1982) focuses on individual memory structures, Leinhardt, Weidman, and Hammond (1987) emphasize socially scripted pattern of behavior in classrooms and mention the mutuality of understanding between teachers and students that is necessary for the enactment of the various scripts. It seems that many kinds of professional scripts are dependent on such mutuality of understanding (e.g., the dentist script, where such mutuality is assumed to exist between dentist and patient).

Moreover, professionals, such as teachers, may develop a collective memory concerning appropriate scripts and MOPs for carrying out their professional activities. Such scripts may be shared among professionals over time and place. This collective memory of scripts might account for the commonality of teachers' scripts in the present study.

MODIFICATIONS OF GENERAL SCRIPTS

Lesson scripts are developed over time and, beyond the shared common elements, they bear the mark of individual past experiences. In the reported scripts of teachers in our study, some of the components included in the scripts are individual routines developed by teachers. Table 10 presents these detailed components of scripts.

Thus, we find welcoming words or singing as personal routines of teachers, constituting parts of the opening of their lessons. Other individual components of scripts are, for instance, reading aloud, dealing with classroom discipline, and summarizing partial topics. The following is a full script of one of the participating retired teachers (the sequence of activities is presented in the form of the teacher's actions):

> Enters the class
> Glances at standing students
> Asks for quiet
> Has them sit down
> Greetings
> Announces topic of lesson
> Writes topic on blackboard (not always)
> Sits down and asks students to take out books and
>   copybooks
> Checks homework (not always)
> Checks knowledge connected to new topic
> Makes some statements concerning new topic
> Asks for quiet or loud reading of text
> Checks for understanding
> Leads discussion
> Corrects misunderstandings and errors
> Presents another level of topic
> Rehearsal
> Keeps discipline
> Assigns homework

Some of the individualized routines in this script are opening greetings, the use of the blackboard for announcing a new topic and quiet or loud reading of text. How do these modifications arise?

As mentioned above, people tend to note and remember mismatches between an experienced event and the generalized structure, thus learning from experience and modifying existing scripts. In comments on their scripts, one teacher, for instance, stated: "I don't assign homework when I don't know how long it will take." This is an example of script modification

Table 10. Detailed Scripts of Lessons Provided by Teachers

Activities	1	2	3	4	5	6	7	8	9	10	11	12	13	14	15	Total
NO. OF SCRIPT																
Smile	•															1
Welcoming	•				•	•				•	•	•		•	•	8
Survey of class									•	•			•			3
Administrative matters								•								1
Singing													•			1
Check of attendance					•	•	•		•	•						5
Checking homework		•	•			•	•		•	•	•					7
Repetition of former material		•				•	•			•	•					5
Continuation of former topic			•													1
Presentation of new topic	•	•		•	•	•	•	•	•	•	•	•	•	•	•	14
Elaboration of new topic					•	•	•		•	•		•	•	•	•	9
Silent reading	•		•	•	•						•					5
Reading aloud	•															1
Teacher lecture		•														1

NO. OF SCRIPT

Activities	1	2	3	4	5	6	7	8	9	10	11	12	13	14	15	Total
Presentation of central problem discussion	●	●	●	●	●	●	●									7
Experimentation								●		●		●				3
Dealing with discipline							●									1
Summing up	●	●		●	●	●		●			●					7
Presentation of review question			●											●		2
Summary of partial topic										●						1
Assigning homework	●	●	●	●	●	●	●	●			●	●	●	●		12
Seat work	●				●	●		●	●					●		5

based on an experienced event that created a problem situation, such as when students were unable to finish their homework. Another teacher said: "The development of the lesson depends on the nature of the topic to be learned." This constitutes another deviation from the generalized script based on this teacher's experiences. Because a certain topic demanded variations in the temporal sequence of lesson components, starting with a discussion instead of presenting the new topic, a modified script was created.

The recalled events of retired teachers reveal the importance of Schank's (1982) "scenes"—structures of memory that provide a physical setting that serves as a basis for reconstruction. In one episode a teacher recounted an incident with a resistant student who refused to write a term essay, claiming that the topics suggested by the teacher did not interest him. The teacher continued:

> The story repeated itself a second time. Once more the boy sat in his place, with his arms crossed over his chest, abstaining demonstratively from writing. I went to him, asked about his behavior, and received the same answer: The topics suggested by you don't interest me.

The teacher went on to tell how she had solved this problem:

> A sudden idea crossed my mind, and I told him: "You know what we'll do. Write a critique of the three topics which I suggested, and voice your opinion, why you don't find them interesting." The boy wrote an interesting essay with many paragraphs, explaining and justifying his rejection of each of the topics. My goal has been reached. He expressed his view in writing in a clear and orderly manner. It is irrelevant that my ego was hurt. He received a good grade.

Event no. 62
Female high school teacher
Middle-class population
Years of practice at the time of the event: 20
Overall years of teaching: 30
Years since retirement: 10

In this fragment of the recalled event we sense how the classroom scene, with students working in their seats according to instructions, has been altered in appropriate ways to be stored in the mind of the teacher and to be recalled in the future. The old structure of classrooms in action has been modified on the basis of a mismatch between the expected generalized structure and the specific experience of the teacher. The new structure included more autonomy for students.

Schank (1982) contends that reminding is a catalyst for generalizations. One learns from experience by collecting similar experiences to make predictions from. Reminding of prior experiences, such as the incident with the reluctant student presented above, is the source of relevant knowledge for this teacher, whose classroom script has been significantly changed by her experience. Her understanding of new experiences, and her ability to deal with problem situations, has been enriched. She has learned from her experience and created a new classroom script to be recalled in the future.

SUMMARY COMMENTS

The analysis of teachers' lesson scripts was based on Schank's (1982) notion of dynamic memory and on the study of teacher routines carried out by Leinhardt, Weidman, and Hammond (1987). Scripts were conceived as representing generalizations of past experiences and serving as guides for planning further actions. Several common elements could be identified in the lesson scripts of retired teachers, but the examination of scripts revealed, as well, individual components that might have developed on the basis of personal past experiences. Deviation from scripts were explained as reflecting their dynamic nature. The analogy between teacher scripts and teacher routines was discussed. The persistent commonalities of teachers' lesson scripts were interpreted as constituting part of the professional collective memory of teachers.

5

What Do the Stories Tell Us? Learning about Teachers and Teaching

> The main point here, however, is not to define teacher lore in terms of somebody's philosophy. It is to relate insights of teachers and to uncover teaching philosophies embedded in teaching practices.
>
> Schubert 1992, p. 9

🌱 THE personal stories recalled by retired teachers are perceived as inherently meaningful to the narrators. Noddings and Witherell (1991) argue that "we learn by both hearing and telling stories. Telling our own stories can be cathartic and liberating. But it is more than that. We discover as we tell and come closer to wisdom" (p. 280). What did the teachers in our study discover? In what ways did they come closer to wisdom? Analysis of their stories may provide some answers to these questions.

This chapter is devoted to the analysis of several of the teachers' remembered stories, focusing on the following main issues:

- What do the stories tell us about insights gained by teachers concerning themselves?
- What have the teachers learned about their students?
- What have they learned about schools and schooling?
- Did the participant teachers reflect on their professional past with satisfaction or with misgivings?

The actual stories are not unidimensional and may yield insights into manifold aspects of teachers' past experiences, viewed through their present-day understanding.

LEARNING ABOUT ONESELF

In my seventh year as a teacher I was asked for the first time to teach math in the fifth grade. I was notified that the superintendent would come to visit my class. He knew me from previous visits to my Bible and language lessons. As this was my first year of teaching math in the fifth grade, I decided to ask the advice of a teacher in a parallel class. This teacher was known as an expert in math teaching and had published math textbooks. The lesson I gave was satisfying, the children participated readily and behaved well. I left the class feeling good about my lesson. In the postlesson meeting the superintendent told me: "I have known you for several years and have visited different lessons in your class. I would like to give you the following advice: Don't use a teaching method that does not suit your personality. Be yourself." At that moment I felt that my eyes had been opened. He had voiced my own hidden feelings. Though the lesson had passed well, I did feel that the method recommended by my colleague did not suit me, "it was not me." The superintendent, who knew me well, sensed this mismatch and commented on it.

Event no. 66
Female high school teacher
Middle-class population
Years of practice at the time of the event: 7
Overall years of teaching: 35
Years since retirement: 8

This event refers to a past experience that served to establish the teacher's sense of her professional identity. The story highlights a dilemma situation for the teacher, who seems to have been torn between contrary viewpoints. On the one hand, she had her own teaching experience to guide her classroom action; on the other hand, she was impressed by the expertise of highly qualified teachers. In retrieving this event from the past, the teacher chose to illuminate a turning point in her career—her insight that she could teach best her "own way."

Several points of interest are embodied in her story. Even with seven years of experience, one can feel as uncertain as a novice when asked to teach a new subject. One can experience satisfaction with one's own performance, and with the students' responses, even while feeling, deep down, that the performance was out of touch with one's own real judgment about how to teach well. Sometimes the response of an external agent is necessary to raise one's awareness of this dilemma and to foster the forming of an explicit sense of professional identity.

This last point raises certain questions: What would have happened, had the superintendent praised the teacher for her use of that specific method of teaching math? What insights about her professional self would she have gained in such a situation? Would she have accepted the "fact" that others "know best?" It seems probable that, had this been the case, she would not have presented it as a recollected event. The unexpectedness of the superintendent's response might have caused this event to be recalled. The degree of consequentiality of the event and its impact of her further experiences may have been considerable, imprinting it on her memory.

Another recalled event focuses on a teacher's learning about herself through her students' responses.

> It was my first lesson in the second grade. After a discussion on breathing and on the functions of lungs, we concluded that smoking was very harmful and may cause dangerous diseases. In the break I lighted, as usual, a cigarette outside the classroom. One of the students cried out: "Teacher, you have told us how harmful smoking is and here you are smoking." "You are right," I replied, and I extinguished the cigarette. Since then I have not smoked. I have learned not to preach one thing and do the opposite. I learned to be very careful about my words.

> Event no. 64
> Female elementary school teacher
> Middle-class population
> Years of practice at the time of the event: 12
> Overall years of teaching: 29
> Years since retirement: 2

This seems to be a rather dramatically reconstructed event. The teacher discusses a watershed-like experience with far-reaching consequences for her professional life, as well as her private life. It is obviously impossible to judge whether this story represents a veritable past experience. Still, it does reveal certain aspects of this teacher's reflection on her professional experiences. She ties her own attempts to conquer smoking to a classroom incident, allowing a student's reproof be her guide. The tone of this narrated event is virtuous and didactic. And yet, what did the teacher learn about herself? That she tended to preach one way and contradicted her preaching through her behavior? Did she become aware of the dangers of such contradictions in classrooms? Perhaps she just learned to be more careful in the future? The text of the event is ambiguous concerning these questions. It is fascinating that this event was brought forward, as it focuses almost totally on the narrator, her problems, her smoking, her difficulties in reconciling her stated beliefs with her overt behavior, and her doubts about being a positive model for her students. Whether she had indeed stopped smoking because of the recalled incident is not so important. What is interesting in this story is the evident self-searching for an ethically sound teaching model.

The previous event seems to carry the message "All's well that ends well." The following event reflects a different situation and highlights the kind of negative self-images that can be related to certain professional experiences.

> In my fifth year of teaching I was transferred to Kiryat-Yam [a small town]. I was homeroom teacher of the third grade. Some of the children had not yet mastered reading and writing. I paid special attention to these students and they showed progress. At the end of the year the results were highly satisfactory. The classes in this school were crowded, forty students in each class. The students came from different backgrounds. Some were children of new immigrants, and others came from well-established homes. This was the first time in my life that I had problems with classroom management and discipline. My confidence in myself was shaken. I was not used to such a situation. I had never before experienced disciplinary prob-

lems. It was extremely difficult for me. On top of that the principal had very specific demands. He used to come into my class to evaluate my use of the blackboard. The school climate was competitive instead of cooperative. Maybe because of the principal's manner it turned out to be a case of "each person for herself."

Event no. 75
Female elementary school teacher
Heterogeneous population
Years of practice at the time of the event: 5
Overall years of teaching: 30
Years since retirement: 7

This teacher's story concerns several factors in the professional lives of teachers that are bound to cause difficulties. The teacher was moved to a new school, she found herself teaching a highly heterogeneous class in which some of the students had not yet mastered the basics. She perceived the school climate as nonsupportive, and highly competitive, and considered herself to be under constant scrutiny by the principal. Her previous successes may have depended to a large extent on a supportive school climate and a less demanding student population. She did not give up; her story tells us that she did succeed with the slower students. And still, the overall tone of this story is sad, almost resigned. The teacher seems to say to herself and to us: "I might not be such a good teacher as I have thought myself to be. This is not wholly my fault, I worked in difficult circumstances." Seven years after her retirement she recalled this event, though it had happened at a fairly early stage of her career, maybe because of its consequentiality for her self-image, or because it had been a first experience with this kind of difficulties. Whatever the reason, her story deserves our full attention because of its inherent sadness and the insights it provides into the shaping of teachers' professional identities through working in difficult circumstances.

All three events have this common feature: that the raising of one's self-awareness stems from personal interactions with significant figures in one's environment. Superintendents, principals, and students can cause teachers to reflect on their beliefs, commitments, and actions, and can change their perceptions for better or for worse. Teachers do not work alone; they are embedded in a social network that shapes their professional selves, with far-reaching consequences for their classroom actions. This social embeddedness may be, in Noddings's (1984) words, "rooted in receptivity, relatedness and responsiveness" (p. 2)—characteristics that are, according to Nodding, "feminine in the deep classical sense."

LEARNING ABOUT STUDENTS

Many of the stories recalled by the participating teachers focused on their students. Sometimes the narrators tell us explicitly what they learned about students, sometimes these insights are implicit in the stories. Let us listen to the voice of one Kindergarten teacher:

> Children try to imitate adults. They hear and understand what goes on in their surroundings. Once the children played in the Doctor's corner. One of the children handed out numbers so the queue would be orderly. I received a number and waited patiently in line. When my turn came this child said: "I am sorry, this is not a women's doctor but a doctor for children only." On another occasion the children built a bus with large wooden blocks. One child played the driver and another the conductor. The conductor found that one of the girls did not have a ticket and decided that she must leave the bus. The girl argued: "The driver is my husband. I am entitled to a free ride."

> Event no. 26
> Kindergarten teacher
> Middle-class population
> Years of practice at the time of the event: 1
> Overall years of teaching: 35
> Years since retirement: 5

Adults are obviously aware that children tend to imitate them. Yet this event sheds light on more-subtle points in this phenomenon. The reporting teacher was struck by the humor of the situation. Kindergarten children noticed, and imitated, some less-desirable features of adult life. The distinctions between various fields of expertise in medicine can confuse patients and cause many inconveniences. People are apt to use personal relations for their own advantage in order to get ahead. It is not the imitation itself that impressed this teacher, but the students' sensitivity to the undercurrents and hidden meanings in their environment. The children's ability to copy adult behavior in an almost cynical manner had a strong impact on the teacher's memory. She may have retold this story to colleagues and friends many times, aiding its recall and retrieval.

Another event concerns a different characteristic of students that seems to have surprised and delighted the narrator.

> I had a student called Avischai. His parents were divorced and his mother raised him as a single parent. Each day she traveled to another, nearby city where she worked. When the child became ill, he stayed by himself the whole day. I used to visit him every day after school, preparing tea and warming his meal. I pitied the child and his mother. Two years later, I had moved to teach in a different location. I returned to my previous school for the graduation ceremony. Avischai's mother approached me and said: "Avischai has grown a plant for you for two years. The flower pot is heavy and I could not carry it with me. Please, as you have your car with you, pass near our home and Avischai will give you the plant." I was extremely moved. This was a very special present for me. The child grew the plant for two years and kept it for me. The present represents the child's attitude and the depth of his feeling.

> Event no. 52
> Elementary school teacher
> Heterogeneous population
> Years of practice at the time of the event: 23
> Overall years of teaching: 35
> Years since retirement: 1

It is interesting to note that this event did not occur early in the teacher's career. When it happened she was an experienced and well-established teacher. Her story portrays mature self-assurance and responsibility. With few sentences the teacher manages to draw the background and to share with her listeners her compassion concerning the circumstances of her student's life. Describing her own actions in helping the family, she sounds matter-of-fact and not overly self-congratulatory. Then comes the emotional and surprising ending. The student did not forget his teacher's help. For two years he tended a plant, waiting for the right opportunity to present it. The teacher seems quite overwhelmed by the perseverance of her former student in his expression of gratitude. Many years of practice had apparently not made her aware of this characteristic of students before then.

Teachers may tend to believe that gifted and mentally disabled children won't find much in common. The following story refutes this belief for one teacher.

> A child of five was accepted to the first grade. He was very handsome but quite small. In the first week of school he showed himself to be different from his schoolmates in behavior and understanding. During lessons he sat on the floor or ran around the room. Once I taught the class about cautious behavior while crossing streets. The young student kept interfering and shouted that he could explain how traffic lights work. I invited him to stand up before the class. He climbed on a chair and explained the color changes in the traffic lights using a poster that hung on the wall. The students listened to his words quietly and I was astonished by his abilities. He was an outstanding student. After this lesson I paid special attention to the boy and discovered another astonishing phenomenon. I saw the student playing regularly in the break with a rather tall chubby girl who had limited mental abilities. She hardly spoke and showed little understanding in class. The two children played happily together in the sand. Though fundamentally different in their intellectual capacities, emotionally they seemed to be close to each other. They did not pay attention to the bell ringing at the end of the break, and used to be late for the lesson. Their clothes were wrinkled and dirty but their eyes shone with plea-

sure. The whole year the boy "assisted" me in my teaching. During the "book" celebration (a special event in which first-year students are presented with their first book), he recited a long poem, "Prayer," by Yalan-Shtekelis. He spoke with deep understanding and feeling, like an adult. The audience was moved to tears, it was an uplifting moment. I remember this event very clearly because I was asked by the principal to repeat the celebration twice more, for the sake of other teachers, superintendents, and student-teachers.

Event no. 93
Elementary school teacher
Middle-class population
Years of practice at the time of the event: 10
Overall years of teaching: 30
Years since retirement: 5

This event concerns a story that unfolds over one year. Several stereotypes about students had been called into question and disproved by the experience of teaching one gifted little boy. Instead of relying on neat pigeonholes to fit students into, the teacher learned about the complex, and sometimes contradictory, coexistence of personal qualities that may lead to a fabric of unaccustomed actions from students. Here was a boy too young for his class, possessing outstanding intellectual abilities, but still behaving partly like a kindergarten student. Though younger than his classmates, he was not shy, but confident in his knowledge and ready to teach others. Yet being an "assistant teacher" did not prevent him from playing as equals with the least able of all the students. The teacher discovered the existence of different kinds of commonalities that allow human beings to interact. In her story she does not tell us explicitly how these experiences have influenced her and changed her views. Her actions reflect her enhanced understanding. She lets the young student be a partner in teaching, while rejoicing with him and his playmate in their joyful play in the school yard. She gives him, the youngest, a major role in a highly regarded celebration. Her actions are vindicated—her decisions are crowned by success. She feels very good about this and remembers the occasion well.

LEARNING ABOUT LIFE IN SCHOOLS

Various events recalled by the retired teachers reflect the linkage between past experiences and deeper understanding of school life. The following event concerns the impact of the sociocultural environment on school culture.

> In the year 1952 I taught in Kibbutz Gesher as an extramural kindergarten teacher (one who is not a member of the kibbutz). The classes were small, twenty children altogether in the kindergarten. It was very difficult for me because I worked in shifts, from morning to noon, from 4 P.M. to 5 P.M. and from 7 P.M. to 8 P.M. [Children of the kibbutz used to be under their teacher's supervision for most of the day.] I worked long hours and that was extremely difficult. The emphasis in the kibbutz kindergarten was on nature studies. This was one of the positive aspects of kibbutz education. We used to visit the cow sheds and the chicken farm, and to drive around on a tractor. The main teaching themes were nature and farming. In the kindergarten the children painted, did needlework, or played with toys—according to their interests and inclination. We did not have "focused time" like in kindergartens in the city. [Focused time is usually devoted to storytelling, guided discussion, show-and-tell activities, etc.] The teaching methods in the kibbutz were quite different. There were very few structured times set aside for teaching. Whoever wished would come and sit near me. Sometimes I told stories or guided a discussion about natural phenomena.

> Event no. 36
> Kindergarten teacher
> Kibbutz population
> Years of practice at the time of the event: 5
> Overall years of teaching: 36
> Years since retirement: 7

Schools tend to exhibit rather uniform features across time and across geographical borders. Teachers may take this uniformity for granted and may react with surprise when moving to a strange and unfamiliar educational environment. The kindergarten teacher recounting her experiences as a kibbutz teacher learned about the variability of school ecologies, about the intimate relationship between societal values and schools. The Israeli kibbutz used to be an agricultural commune. Nature and environment were highly valued. Many kibbutz schools adhered to a progressive educational ideology, with students having a voice in determining their curriculum. The narrator does not elaborate on these issues, but her story identifies some of the main features of kibbutz education.

Still another component of school life is revealed in this story. Zerubavel (1981) distinguishes between public time and private time as possible expressions of sociotemporal dimensions. Public time is that part of one's day in which one is on call for professional and occupational purposes. During private-time segments, one is not expected to carry out work obligations. In general, teachers are on public time during school hours only, but in the kibbutz public time may be spread out over the whole day. Because of the close personal relationships in small communities, like a kibbutz, parents and students may feel free to approach the teachers during all hours, leaving them almost no private time. The teacher remembering her experiences as a kindergarten teacher in a kibbutz refers to the difficulty of adapting to such demands.

Another teacher recalls her experiences when working as a school principal:

> The larger the teaching staff, the less cooperation one finds. The teachers' lounge in such schools may be a fairly tolerant place, but lacks real friendships among teachers. Groups of teachers are formed which tend to become antagonistic and hostile. It becomes very difficult to engage all teachers in a common task. Sometimes I heard teachers insult and hurt each other. I used to be quite disappointed after meetings of the pedagogic school council. Some of the teachers supported my efforts, others were in constant opposition. There were open confrontations, and sometimes hidden resistance. It was extremely difficult to implement innovation and change. As a principal I used to

insist that parallel classes used the same textbooks. This meant that similar teaching strategies were going to be used, for instance, in math teaching. It was necessary to require that all teachers participate in in-service courses and prepare appropriate teaching aids. Some teachers did so willingly, some did it as a favor for me, and some just went along. When their efforts yielded higher achievement, the teachers were satisfied. Sometimes we found that a certain teaching strategy did not work, and we had to adopt a new one. Teachers work under great pressure, but it is not desirable to remain locked in one mode of teaching. When I was a principal I felt alone in my educational efforts. There were many heated discussions in the teachers' lounge concerning the timetable, the allocation of classes, and teacher meetings.

Event no. 78
Elementary schoolteacher and principal
Middle-class population
Years of practice at the time of the event: 20
Overall years of teaching: 30
Years since retirement: 7

The narrator starts her story with some general comments on life in schools, focusing on conflicts between teachers and principals and on the tensions in teachers' lounges. She describes these phenomena from the viewpoint of a principal who is eager to implement innovations in her school and who is disappointed when teachers do not cooperate fully in her plans. The story moves on to an example of teaching math according to specific textbooks. The story itself has the flavor of an outburst of long-kept grievances, especially about the situation in the teachers' lounge, which has left such bitter memories. This is a case of presenting problems concerning change in schools, by someone whose past experiences have taught her not to expect too much cooperation from teachers.

The following event provides insights into the nature of the relationship between principal and teachers from the teacher's point of view.

Our school, like all schools, maintained certain regulations. It was forbidden to bring penknives to school. One student, his name was Schmueli, was found to have a penknife and was sent to the principal's office. The principal reprimanded Schmueli, who happened to be a good student and a good kid. He was told that if he ever brought his penknife to school he would be sent home and would have to return with his parents. Since then the boy had not brought the penknife with him. At the end-of-term teachers' meeting concerning grades [in Israel all class teachers meet to discuss their students' term-grades], the principal claimed that the student deserved a poor grade in classroom behavior. The principal managed to enforce his opinion in spite of the opposition of the homeroom teacher and the other teachers of this class. The same scenario repeated itself in the second term. The principal continued to argue that such a misdemeanor had to receive appropriate punishment in the form of a low grade. In a former teachers' meeting it had been decided that the principal would have no veto rights on grades. A compromise was reached, and the student received an average grade. In one of the next meetings teachers wanted to reopen the issue, but the principal refused to discuss the topic. I believe that the reason for his stubbornness was that he lacked jurisdiction over grades in subject-matter areas, like math or phys ed., therefore he wanted to have powers of decisions concerning grades in students' behavior. There were many confrontations with the principal over this matter. I am still angry about this incident. All teachers expressed great anger.

Event no. 38
Male high school teacher
Heterogeneous population
Years of practice at the time of the event: 28
Overall years of teaching: 30
Years since retirement: 3

This story reflects the power structure and power struggles in school. It is a recollection of a fairly recent event that still causes feelings of great anger. One gets a picture of a school that is divided between teachers and the principal, with the teachers defending their students against an overly strict disciplinarian. It may well be that the narrator found the overall school climate to be disturbing and unpleasant; his story reflects such feelings. It is interesting that of the many possible recollections, this teacher chose to tell a story of interpersonal strife in school. The specific story tells us implicitly about his more liberal pedagogical beliefs and about his views concerning teacher autonomy versus the decision-making power of principals.

LOOKING BACK WITH SATISFACTION

When talking with teachers, we often hear about the difficulties of being a teacher. Complaints may concern unruly classes, long hours of preparation, testing, grading, stern principals, demanding parents, and low salaries. How do retired teachers, who are no longer involved in teachers' daily struggles, view their past experiences? When listening to their voices, do we hear disappointment, misgivings, dissatisfaction? Do we get the impression that these teachers regret their past and are unhappy with the results of their professional efforts? Or do teachers look back with a sense of satisfaction, a sense of work done well? Do teachers convey feelings of having played an important role in the lives of their students, of having contributed to society?

Many of the participating teachers in this study seem to view their professional past with deep satisfaction. Sometimes this satisfaction expresses itself in brief evaluative statements, such as these: "At the end of the year the results were highly satisfactory" (Event no. 75); "We taught many hours and stayed overtime to help the weak students with their homework. These additional teaching hours helped the weaker students and improved their achievements" (Event no. 51).

Sometimes the recalled event reflects a sense of educational accomplishment beyond successful achievement tests. For instance: "I organized a performance in the second grade.

This happened eight years ago. The theme was 'my country.' I wrote the text with the children. Many songs, stories, proverbs, landscapes were part of the performance. We sang and danced. The performance was so moving and successful that we repeated it at the end-of-term ceremony for graduates. It gave us a wonderful feeling" (Event no. 115). These statements link success with teachers' hard work. Their efforts are perceived as yielding positive results, and the teachers feel rewarded and express their satisfaction.

Teachers may present their successful educational strategy, as in the following event reported by a kindergarten teacher.

> I had a student who used to hit his classmates. It turned out that he suffered physical abuse at home. I tried to give him, as well as other children who had behavior problems, prizes for good behavior. My goal was to encourage these children and provide positive reinforcement. This proved to be a highly successful strategy.
>
> Event no. 21
> Kindergarten teacher
> Middle-class population
> Years of practice at the time of the event: unknown
> Overall years of teaching: 31
> Years since retirement: 2

The message embedded in this event seems to be that appropriate teaching strategies help one overcome serious difficulties encountered in practice—there is no need for despair, it is possible to succeed even in difficult situations.

Rewards of teaching may be experienced many years after one's students leave school. Another kindergarten teacher tells the following story:

> Having worked with utmost devotion, one may remember many things. When I meet a former student of mine I remember many details, how a child came to kindergarten, what had happened to him or her. Some of my former students are forty-seven years old, and still they remember me. Two months ago I

stood in line in the bank. In front of me stood a tall
handsome man. He turned to me: "Hi, I am Eyal." I
was very excited: "I remember you, sitting in my kindergarten, very serious, working on puzzles and crying when someone disturbed you. What do you do?"
"I am a sports coach." Remembering him in kindergarten, I could not believe it. I always thought that he
would become a scientist. It seems that people change.
I may have been wrong in my perception.

Event no. 39
Kindergarten teacher
Heterogeneous population
Years of practice at the time of the event: after retirement
Overall years of teaching: 33
Years since retirement: 5

Remembering students and being remembered by them is highly
gratifying for teachers, and a measure of their success. Even
when the specific memory is not validated, as in the event
above, the whole experience is perceived as positive and
rewarding.

The more difficult the teaching circumstances, the more
pronounced is a teacher's sense of achievement. An elementary
school teacher tells about her activities in coping with a heterogeneous class:

> new immigrants, old-timers, children from broken
> homes. . . . It was very difficult to teach this class
> because of the large differences between the students.
> I had to match my teaching to children at different
> levels of knowledge. I used to prepare varied plans
> and learning activities, and different worksheets.
> (Event no. 51)

Improved achievement was this teacher's reward. She felt that
she had accomplished a most important societal task—closing
the gap between newcomers and children coming from well-
established homes.

What might account for this apparent sense of satisfaction
that characterizes many of the recalled events? One of the most

obvious explanations concerns people's tendency to recall successful experiences rather than failures (Kihlstrom 1981). The Pollyanna principle has been demonstrated by Matlin and Stang (1978) to favor recall of positive and successful events. Pleasant events might be more salient to the narrator who tries to share past experiences with others. It may seem more constructive to share success stories than to paint gloomy pictures of the past.

There are other factors that might account for the teachers' positive views. All the participants in this study were retired teachers who had been asked to recollect a professional event from their past. In a sense they were engaged in reviewing this past. It seems reasonable and rational that many would prefer a positive "summing up," because the alternative would be too painful. They had devoted a lifetime to teaching and probably could not bear to perceive this expenditure of time, energy, and efforts as wasteful and unproductive. In this context one has to take into consideration the process of self-selection by the participants. It may well be that retired teachers who looked back with anger and pain were not ready to share their memories with researchers.

Moreover, many of the stories convey a strong feeling of hope, as difficulties are shown to have been overcome, yielding positive, even exciting, educational results. The retired teachers seem to send a message to other teachers—namely: What we strive for can be achieved, don't lose your hopes, and don't lower your expectations.

Last but not least, we have to consider the special social and historical context of these stories. Most of the participating teachers had started their professional careers in the difficult first years of the State of Israel. These were years of massive immigration of people from neighboring states in the Middle East and from North Africa. Many of the immigrants from Europe were Holocaust survivors. Resources, even buildings and textbooks, were minimal, and expectations were high. The major task of the educational system was to provide all children, those of newcomers and those of well-established citizens, with a sound and useful education. Most teachers were unprepared for this task, and yet they managed to fulfill their role. In spite of many failures and mistakes, the educational story of Israel reveals a steady process toward a more egalitarian and equitable system. Kindergarten and elementary school teachers played a major role in this process. Teachers' narratives reflect their awareness of this role and their pride in their professional accomplishments.

SUMMARY COMMENTS

Bruner (1986) exmphasizes the importance of stories in under-standing oneself and one's culture. The stories referred to in this chapter reveal how retired teachers understand themselves as teachers, and how they learned about students and the school culture, with all its messages of power and control.

Awareness of self is to be found in retired teachers' overall positive view of their past careers. They tell their audience about the personal and societal significance of the teaching profession, with its ongoing ethical challenges. Implicit in their stories is a voice that seems to cry out: "It was worth to make all these efforts, we did make a difference."

6

Stories, Stories: The Tales of Teachers' Memories

The only way to discover the limits of the possible is to go beyond them to the impossible.
Clarke's Law (Dickson 1978, p. 27)

🌱 WHEN asked to recollect events from their professional past, the retired teachers told their stories in the form of coherent texts. According to Elbaz (1991), tellers strive to create coherent meaning in their stories. The notion of story "evokes an image of a community of listeners" (p. 6), for whom this meaning had been created. Stories can be interpreted in different ways in order to reveal their meaning. Up to this point teachers' recollections were analyzed from the perspective of different content areas and the impact of contextual characteristics on their stories. Interpretation of teachers' stories led to insights into knowledge teachers gained about themselves, their students, and the life of schools. Three additional perspectives for analysis of retired teachers' stories are employed herewith:

- The rhetorical macrostructure of the text
- The "point of view" reflected in the story
- The stylistic characteristics of the text

These perspectives provide further insights into the nature of teachers' memories. We will now further elaborate these and their implications for the understanding of teachers' professional memories.

THE RHETORICAL MACROSTRUCTURES OF THE STORIES

All the events recalled by retired teachers in this study were told by a protagonist-narrator who retrieved episodes from the past. The narrator's voice is heard throughout the story, telling about her or his experiences, actions, and feelings. In the various episodes the narrators appear as active figures, reflecting on their situation, solving problems, learning from experience, changing and developing as professionals. The centrality of the narrator in the recalled events is congruent with the finding of Fitzgerald (1988). Almost all the memories of respondents in his study "were written in the form of a first person narrative and presented a coherent story. Even nationally important events tended to be woven into stories of what the person telling the story did" (p. 265). The narrator may structure and shape the story in diverse ways: The rhetorical structure of the documented events may be perceived as creating its coherence. Coherence is defined as the logical and rhetorical features that transform a series of statements into a unified text (Nir 1984). Van Dijk (1980) states that "intuitively, coherence is a semantic property of discourses, based on the interpretation of each individual sentence relative to the interpretation of other sentences. . . . Sentences or propositions in a discourse may form a coherent discourse, however, even if they are not all connected to every other sentence or proposition" (p. 93).

Elbaz (1991) claims, "If the story achieves a unity or wholeness, it is because the teller has done so, not because unity has been found to inhere in the stuff itself" (p. 5). The narrators may arrange matters in a consistent story line that conveys a sense of purposeful coherence. The coherence of stories can be achieved by temporal sequence, causal connections, descriptive structures, as well as by other means for organizing parts of a text into a meaningful whole. The rhetorical structure of a story as a coherent entity is analyzed herewith using the following three categories: organization of sequence, beginnings, endings.

Organization of sequence, the order in which events occur in the reported story, can be determined by different principles. A common organizing principle is *chronological connection.* In cases where this principle was applied, the order of events in the story is presented as conforming to the order of events in the original experience. The following is an example of such a story:

> In the twelfth year of practice, in 1966, I taught in a
> school in Nveh-Shaanan [a quarter of Haifa]. In the

beginning there was a feeling of creating in a vacuum. We started to teach in an unfinished building, without electricity and phones. There was no road leading to the school and no school yards. Still, we opened the school. When the yard was finished we celebrated. When the first road was paved we celebrated. There was a sense of togetherness, of a unified school. Over time the school grew. Many new immigrants arrived and new houses were built. The immigrants did not know any Hebrew. Somehow they learned and progressed. Some excelled in their studies. They received remedial lessons throughout the year. This was a difficult time. We had to explain everything by using our hands and feet.

Event no. 77
Female elementary school teacher
Heterogeneous population
Years of practice at the time of the event: 12
Overall years of teaching: 30
Years since retirement: 7

The narrator used a time line to report on her experiences, noting the time and place, which starts the flow of memories. One event leads to another, accompanied by references to the emotional climate of the times, and to personal feelings. The last sentences focus on the nature of the hardships experienced by the narrator. It is interesting to note that in this case the earlier days, which were characterized by many physical adversities, were perceived as happy times, whereas later developments of pedagogical difficulties were remembered as "difficult times." This change might be related to the fact that it was apparently easier for this teacher to cope with passing environmental problems, which were not dependent on her and were dealt with by the local authorities, than to confront a student population with whom she had grave communication difficulties, feeling the lack of skills to deal with the situation. The story stops abruptly, without a clear "resolved ending," with no settling of the obvious dilemmas of teaching in an unknown cultural territory, though the teacher notes that "somehow they learned."

Chronological connections provide a natural structure for creating a coherent story, because "memories are stored within a temporal frame of reference and are linked to landmark events in public life and in personal life" (Cohen 1989, p. 119). In the story presented above, the professional events are linked to public events, namely, the massive project of building living quarters for new immigrants. The temporal frame of reference for storing memories is reflected in the process of free recall (Linton 1986). In Linton's research on accessing the contents of her own memory, she found that most of her recall process involved chronological searches. In about a quarter of all events recalled by teachers, chronological connections were used as the basic structure of the stories.

Causal connections constitute another important mode of creating a coherent story. This mode was used by the participant teachers to the same extent as chronological connections. Events in the story develop on the basis of cause-and-effect relationships. The following episode serves as an example:

> In 1980 we studied a story called "A Blind Girl." A student-teacher sat in class and listened to the lesson. The children were spellbound and very attentive. Suddenly the door opened and the principal stormed in. "Who are the students on cleaning duty?" she cried. "Is that the way to sweep the classroom floor?" She insisted that the students sweep the room in the middle of the lesson. The whole lesson was destroyed. This had been a well-structured and fascinating lesson. All the students had been attentive and involved. With one strike the interesting lesson was destroyed.
>
> Event no. 82
> Female high school teacher
> Middle-class population
> Years of practice at the time of the event: 19
> Overall years of teaching: 26
> Years since retirement: 3

This story is structured completely around the notion of cause and effect: The actions of the principal disrupt a successful lesson. This episode can be read as involving moral aspects and value judgments, which convey several hidden messages about classroom causality. First, the notion of a "good" lesson entails the complete absorption and engagement of students. There is an assumed causal relationship between the theme of the lesson, the act of good teaching, and the impact on students. Outside and managerial considerations, such as attention to the cleanliness of the floor, especially if these are voiced by an agent who is not part of the classroom community, are perceived as causing havoc with the lesson. Moreover, the pedagogical balance of the lesson is considered to be highly fragile. One act of intrusion can cause disruption and breakdown of a delicate web of teaching and learning.

The student-teacher as classroom observer plays a role in the unfolding drama. Her presence seems to cause the teacher to feel more intensively the threat to her autonomy and professionalism evoked by the principal's act of interference.

The importance of causal reasoning in memory retrieval strategies has been emphasized by Reiser, Black and Kalamanides (1986). They claim that "as a consequence of the central role that causal representation play in comprehension, the components of the memory representation for an experience are constructed using causal knowledge and are connected to these planning structures in memory" (p. 117). In remembering their past professional experiences, teachers tell their audiences stories that reflect these causal structures.

Research on memory of events in young children (Slackman, Hudson, and Fivush 1986) has shown that even very young children perceive causality in events. This perception is considered to be a necessary stage in the development of the understanding of causality. "Event structure may initially function as an implicit scaffold. Once event relations are fully understood, the child is freed to transform and manipulate event sequences by accessing knowledge about cause and effect contingencies" (p. 68). In a similar manner, teachers' knowledge about the likelihood of cause-and-effect phenomena in their classrooms may constitute one possible way of transforming experience into professional knowledge through the decontextualization and abstraction of knowledge of causal relations from familiar event sequences.

Another way of creating story coherence is through *contrastive connections*. The text is organized on the basis of contrasting persons, situations, or attitudes. The juxtaposition of story elements creates a conceptual relationship between these elements and serves the achievement of a coherent text. For example the following event which has been presented above (chapter 2) as exemplifying interpersonal relationships:

> After three years, in 1972, I was working in Tira. The supervisor there was a very harsh and frightening woman. She used to appear in my dreams like a witch. She admired my work but begrudged me my success. Once she arrived at my kindergarten with a whole group of visitors. I held a tray with apples in my hands. When I saw her the tray slipped out of my hands and the apples scattered on the floor. Once she screamed at me demanding why I did not have a full list of attendance in my diary. She made me cry. I went to another supervisor in order to resign. I put the keys of the kindergarten on his desk and told him: "I resign." I burst out crying: "I cannot stand this evil supervisor any longer." Sometime later a new supervisor arrived. She was wonderful, supported me greatly, helped me with good advice and warm friendship, thus restoring the supervisor–kindergarten teacher relationship. All-new projects were implemented in my kindergarten. Over many years student-teachers and visitors from abroad used to visit my kindergarten.

Event no. 28
Female kindergarten teacher
Lower-class population
Years of practice at the time of the event: 4
Overall years of teaching: 12
Years since retirement: 10

Contrasting two dissimilar supervisors links the two parts of the story together while shedding light on the nature of this kindergarten teacher's experiences with her supervisors. The audience is moved to empathy with the narrator and to an understanding of her perceptions of the situations.

Contrasting connections represent one mode of coherent storytelling and were used in about 10 percent of all events. The contrasting mode can be very important in shaping teachers' knowledge. Fitzgerald (1988) claims that a set of stories can define who we are in narrative, rather than declarative, terms. The story about two different supervisors imposes an understandable order in the complex domain of interpersonal relations with one's superiors in the educational system. The emphasis of this recalled event is on the integration of the teacher's feelings and actions. One supervisor made this teacher feel unwanted, deskilled, and angry. These feelings expressed themselves in her inability to act as usual. On the other hand, the supportive supervisor created an atmosphere of mutual trust and the opportunity for trying out new projects.

Sometimes the story depends on a *descriptive structure,* focusing on the description of a place, a social situation, a person, and so forth. For instance:

> I was sent to teach in the village A.K. near Tivon. I was nineteen years old; luckily my best girlfriend worked in the same school. It was an appalling place. The intercity bus did not reach the village. I would get off the bus on the highway and wait for the local bus to take me to the nearest forest. From there my friend and I would walk on a sandy trail until we reached the village. We had to walk along an unpaved footpath to reach the school, which was situated on a distant hill. The building was old and lacked doors and windows. Two classes had no rooms, and we used to study beneath the trees in the yard. I would take my students outside, teaching them as much as I could. Sometimes, in the heat of summer, I would take them to a nearby stream. We would put our feet in the cool water, rest sometimes, drink from the stream, and return to school refreshed.

Event no. 63
Female elementary school teacher
Lower-class population
Years of practice at the time of the event: 1
Overall years of teaching: 18
Years since retirement: 2

In this episode the narrator depends on descriptive details to create a vivid image of a school in the distant past. There is no plot in the story, and yet one gets a sense of the environment and the atmosphere of a school in extremely distressing condition. Because of the calm, almost pastoral, descriptive tone of this story, with no complaints voiced, and no reference to difficulties in teaching in such circumstances, the general message is one of looking back with nostalgia to the very first professional experiences, in spite of the appalling circumstances.

A very different story uses a deductive structure to move the audience from a *generalized statement to particular instances* that function as supportive details, clarifying or exemplifying the generalization, as reflected in the following event:

> Teachers can strengthen and enhance the abilities of their students, but they can also destroy them completely. In the first elementary grades, teachers' knowledge is less important than their character and empathy with students. For instance: In my twelfth year of teaching I was the homeroom teacher of a third grade. One of the students had great difficulties in learning to read. His former homeroom teachers, in the second grade, referred to him as "a piece of furniture in the classroom." I was shocked by her words. I devoted special attention to this student and tried to encourage him. After the other students had read aloud from the posters around the room, I told this student to read them again, which he succeeded in doing. Sometimes I gave him extra time to prepare himself ahead of the other students to read a portion of text. The next day he would be able to read it fluently. In this manner I encouraged him over the whole year and even raised his status among the other children. I engaged him in various class activities—handing out learning materials, being responsible for the classroom cupboard, etc. After many years I met him and he reminded me of encouraging him and asking him to fulfill different functions in class. He told me that he would never forget these experiences. I was very happy to hear his words. They gave meaning to my life, they made my day. It is important to note that even in the higher grades he was not

considered to be a weak student. He was an average student.

Event no. 79
Female elementary school teacher
Heterogeneous population
Years of practice at the time of the event: 12
Overall years of teaching: 30
Years since retirement: 7

The narrator focuses on an educational principle: She considers the crucial major role that teachers' actions play in determining the academic and social development of their students. The intensity with which she recalls the details of her own practice concerning one third-grade student shows that this principle constitutes her guiding educational philosophy. The elaboration of activities enables her audience to understand explicitly what she meant by her opening general statement. Moreover, the story has a happy ending—the teacher is confirmed in her belief and shares this validation with us. It is as if the narrator had searched her professional memories to find the one event that captures the whole story of her practice, its guiding principle, the appropriate details of classroom actions, and the evidence for the validity of her approach. The movement from generalized statements to particular instances may be understood to reflect the "nesting" theory (Neisser 1986) of the structure of memory.

According to Neisser, "events defined at one level of analysis may themselves be constituents of other, larger events. This 'nested' structure appears not only in the events themselves but also in the way they are experienced and remembered. . . . Recalling an experienced event is a matter not of reviving a single record but of moving appropriately among nested levels of structure" (p. 71).

Neisser sees similarity between the uses of the concept of nesting in ecological descriptions of the real world and its uses in understanding the structure of memories. Things are components of other things, without any clear hierarchy, because of the many transitions and overlaps. The nested structure of memories plays a crucial role in their recall. "There are links between the levels: When one of them becomes active in recall I can recall others that are nested inside it, or in which it is nested. Most recall moves either downward from context or upwards from particulars" (Neisser 1986, p. 77).

Neisser's "nesting" theory of autobiographical memory may have implications for the study of teachers' memories and might serve to explain individual styles of recall, whether downward from context or upward from particulars.

In several documented episodes the flow of memories reflects *free association,* and the story lacks clear coherence. For instance:

> When I worked in Acre in 1967, one teacher, who taught in a parallel class, was on maternity leave. Student-teachers were called in to help, but I was responsible for the two second grades. The student-teachers helped me with teaching, and I acted as their mentor. The other teacher and I used to work together, we taught the same content and used the same materials. The difference was in the presentation of the material, which depended on the teacher's character. We worked cooperatively, one enriching the other's practice. We had wonderful relations with the principal, who was a new immigrant, an able administrator and a wizard in interpersonal relationships. I was ready to do everything. The school climate was outstanding. When I was in my ninth month of pregnancy, I organized a Pentecost festival for the whole school, including the parents. Everyone believed they should do their utmost. The children used newspapers to wrap their copybooks. I keep everything, the students' copybooks, their assignments, my lesson plans.
>
> Event no. 74
> Female elementary school teacher
> Lower-class population
> Years of practice at the time of the event: 13
> Overall years of teaching: 30
> Years since retirement: 7

The process of retrieval of professional memories from the past leads this narrator from one episode to the other, based on free associations. Telling about the student-teachers, who acted as teacher aides, reminds her of her cooperation with other teachers, which in turn reminds her of her relationship with the principal. She moves then to an episode during her pregnancy that serves as an example for the general attitude of teachers' commitment to the school. The statement about students' using newspapers for wrapping their copybooks sheds some light on the poverty of the student population and can be interpreted as providing the context for the teachers' devotion. Thinking about copybooks leads us to the concluding sentence, which ties the past to the present, as the copybooks are still kept by this teacher. The story lacks coherence, but the audience does get a sense of this teacher's past practice and the centrality of personal relationships in her professional life. Through what appears to be a random reference to various episodes, we get to know this teacher and her story of being a teacher, which is not finished though she stopped teaching long ago. By telling us that she still keeps her students' copybooks and assignments, and even her lesson plans, she seems to declare that she still defines herself as a teacher, ready to teach.

Beginnings

"Beginnings and endings are always crucial to the telling of a tale or the construction of a narrative unit" (Hayman and Rabkin 1974, p. 107). Narrators can choose different ways to begin their stories. One way to start a story is to introduce the audience to the main elements of the story, the main actors, the time and locality, the social and geographical environment. Sternberg (1974) states that

> it is the function of the exposition to introduce the reader into an unfamiliar world, the fictive world of the story, by providing him with the general and specific background information indispensable to the understanding of what happens in it. There are some pieces of information, the number and nature of which

varies from one work to another, that the reader cannot do without. He must usually be informed, for instance, of the time and place of the action; of the
nature of the peculiar fictive world projected by the
work, or, in other words, of the canons of probability
operating in it; of the history, the appearance, the
traits and habitual behavior of some of the dramatis
personae; and of the relations between them. This ex-
positional information the author is obliged to communicate to the reader in one way or another. (pp. 25–26)

Here are some examples of kindergarten teachers' story
beginnings in the form of exposition:

In the year 1956 I worked in Acre. The population
was mixed, residents and new immigrants. Most immigrants had come from Europe and their socioeconomic level was very low. (Event no. 2)

In the year 1956 I taught in a kindergarten in a
settlement of new immigrants. All the children had
come from North Africa. They did not know one word
of Hebrew. (Event no. 11)

Some children in our kindergarten came from a home
for preschoolers. These were children from malfunc-
tioning families and had many problems. One of the
children was "Schalom," he was extremely difficult!
(Event no. 25)

I had a very good class. One of the students was
exceptionally bright, but mischievous and a trouble-
maker. His name was Gil. (Event no. 68)

Mentioning the time of the event and its physical location
contributes to understanding the described incidents. The difficulties and problems encountered by the narrators stem in
part from the temporal and social features of the situation.
Often one finds a relationship between time and place of events.
For instance, during the time of massive immigration into Israel, in the first years after the establishment of the State of

Israel, many immigrants lived in provisional settlements called "Maabarot" (singular: Maabara), in tents or huts. The locality and its inhabitants played a significant role in determining the character of the teaching situation and the perceptions of teachers. Working in a Maabara, teachers may have felt alienated, lonely, and powerless. The professional goals and strategies in well-established locations were very different from those in settlements of new immigrants. In the latter the main emphasis was on language acquisition and on achievement in the "basics"— reading, comprehension, and arithmetic. The exposition of the story is essential for the audience to understand what happens in it, what difficulties were encountered by the narrators, and what their dilemmas were.

Exposition was by far the mode most frequently chosen by the teachers for beginning their stories.

In some of the teachers' memories one finds *framed beginnings*—the same statements are repeated in the beginning and the end of the story, creating a verbal framework for it. For instance:

Beginning: "I remember the most beautiful party I have ever organized."
End: "I believe that was one of the most beautiful parties planned by me." (Event no. 40)

Beginning: "All through my teaching career my conversations with students used to move me."
End: "All along I had a feeling of great excitement." (Event no. 22)

The framing of a story created a cyclical structure indicating stability and lack of change. Rendering a recalled event in this form can be interpreted as an indication of a teacher's sense of closure, or finality of professional involvement—a kind of summing up.

The narrator might choose a *dramatic beginning*, in the form of direct speech. Such an opening involves the audience in the scene of the transactions taking place in the story. It allows the narrator to present the actions instead of talking about them. A dramatic beginning arouses curiosity and interest. For instance:

"Teacher, you'd better beat him. Only a beating will
stop his troublemaking. That is the way he is treated
at home, and the other teachers hit him as well." I
was stunned. (Event no. 98)

Such a beginning is bound to raise our interest in the
story. Dramatic beginnings provide an example for the reconstruction of personal memories. The memories are not recent,
and the purpose of recall is to tell a tale about them. The story
format may guide the process of this reconstruction. Construction of one's memories may be strongly influenced by the conventions of narrative (Spence 1982). This reconstruction does
not necessarily detract from the validity of one's memories. "If
most autobiographical memories are reconstructions, they are
not often exact in detail event though memories are true in the
sense of maintaining the integrity and gist of past events"
(Barclay 1986, p. 82).

Endings

Matching the ending of a story to the flow of its content com-
pletes its coherent structure. In the memories of participant
teachers a common way of ending, in about 50 percent of all
stories, was through a narrative clause that concluded the story
they chose to tell. The following are some examples:

The connection with parents became like family relations. They helped me as much as they could. (Event
no. 30)

The student started to come to school regularly and
finished the year successfully. (Event no. 96)

At the end of the year the situation improved as the
students had learned the language. (Event no. 11)

The police succeeded in arresting a gang of thieves
who studied at our school. (Event no. 120)

Many times a happy ending concludes the story of a remembered professional event. This seems to be a common phenomenon in personal memories.

Drawing conclusions, devising rules, pointing to the moral of a tale are other ways to end a story. For instance:

> I have learned not to preach one thing and do the opposite. I learned to be careful about my words. (Event no. 64)

> The conditions described above forced me to reach the conclusion that there can be no achievements without effort. (Event no. 107)

Event no. 7, about Isri who caught his fingers in the classroom door, ends with a series of conclusions as follows:

> I learned several things from this event concerning the following issues:
>
> 1. What is the appropriate place for a wall newspaper?
> 2. How to overcome sudden anger? How to consider the appropriate reaction to students' behavior?
> 3. How to provide maximum safety in the classroom?
> 4. A person may be understood not only by his charity, his anger, and his drinking habits (an ancient Hebrew saying), but also by his behavior when in pain. I assume that much more may be learned from the event.

These endings are similar to the kinds of generalizing commentary used by authors of novels. According to Booth (1961), many authors tend to incorporate direct generalizing comments in their works, though in other cases the task of generalization might be left entirely to the reader. Teachers who share their past experiences with an imagined audience may wish to clarify explicitly the insights they gained. These generalized endings may reflect a nested structure of memory (Neisser 1986) moving upward from particulars.

Different kinds of knowledge are reflected in these generalized endings. They might be in the form of rules of practice—for instance, not to hang a poster near the classroom door (Hannah's story). Sometimes a principle of practice is evoked, like "Without effort there is no achievement" (Event no. 107). Often the generalization bears strong moral tones. Hansen (1992) claims that "moral education can be conceived as an everyday dimension of classroom interaction" (p. 346). Teachers may be able to express their moral framework more clearly when relating to their professional experiences in the past than they were able to when they were in the classroom. Isri's teacher, Hannah, seemed to have consolidated her professional knowledge and her moral convictions concerning schooling, through the process of looking back at years of educational practice. She shared her insights with a potential audience of educators, eager to be articulate and explicit so that her intended messages would be clear.

A *present-time perspective* is another possible way of ending one's story. For instance:

> Even today this issue makes me very angry. (Event no. 88)

> Today I am certain that the inspector was wrong. (Event no. 87)

> When I meet my former students today, we kiss and talk about the past. They are glad to see me. (Event no. 1)

This mode of closing one's tale can be interpreted as reflecting the continuing importance of the remembered event that is still very much on the mind of the narrator. It may be seen as a literary device that bridges the past and present.

An interesting literary mode adopted by some teachers is the *surprise ending.* The sudden, unexpected turn of events provides the story with new and different meaning, as exemplified by the following recorded memory:

> In the year 1960 I worked in Acre, in the eighth grade of a school that was situated at the outskirts of the town. The class was very heterogeneous, children of normal learning abilities who had behavioral disorders studied with children with a variety of learning disabilities. One thirteen-year-old boy was still unable to read. These were the years after the great immigration, and most students were new immigrants

who had come to Israel as young children. I was a homeroom teacher of the eighth grade. There were only fifteen students in the class because of their special difficulties. One of the students was 6 feet tall, he was somewhat retarded, and his manner of speaking was strange. One day, during the break, I was standing beside a friend, a colleague who was pregnant. The student was extremely rude to my friend, and without thinking I hit him in his face. The student reacted immediately and shouted several times: "I'll kill you, I'll kill you." His voice was heard all over the school yard, and many students gathered around us. I was mortally afraid, but recovered my senses because I answered: "OK, kill me." He was completely stunned, kept walking around the yard repeating: "Teacher, I'll kill you." The break was over and we returned to our classroom, the boy was very quiet. I felt the admiration of the students. The next day the student came to school accompanied by his parents. I thought to myself: "Here it comes." The father approached me and said: "Our son came home yesterday and told us that you had hit him in his face. He wanted us to meet you, the courageous teacher, because he admires you so much."

Event no. 65
Female elementary school teacher
Lower-class population
Years of practice at the time of the event: 4
Overall years of teaching: 30
Years since retirement: 3

The surprising ending closes the detailed story and is contrary to our expectations. It was to be expected that hitting a student would cause strong condemnation by his parents and by other members of the school community. The guilt feelings of the teacher about her impulsive and illegal action are reflected in her efforts to justify her deed by describing the difficult situation and by mentioning the pregnancy of her colleague, which serves as an excuse. It might be that in remembering this painful event the narrator has blocked other less favorable

reactions—for instance, from the principal and from her colleagues. In the end she becomes a hero to her class.

POINT OF VIEW

Point of view in personal memories has been studied by various
researchers. Nigro and Neisser (1983) distinguish between the
perspective of an observer, on the one hand, and one's own
"field perspective," on the other hand. In some memories one
seems to be looking at the situation from an external vantage
point. In other cases the recalled scene is seen from one's own
position, the narrator adopts the point of view of the original
situation.

Nigro and Neisser (1983) found that this qualitative feature of personal memories, the perspective from which they are
recalled, may be related to characteristics of the original event,
to one's purpose in recalling that event, and to the interval
between recall and the original experience. In their studies they
found a preponderance of field memories. A focus on feelings
seems to lead to more field memories. According to Nigro and
Neisser (1983), people who are given no special directions generally focus on their own feelings in remembering an event.

Booth (1961), in writing about the rhetoric of fiction, distinguishes between an "intrusive" and an "unintrusive" narrator. Intrusive narrators express their attitudes and feelings
concerning the events and characters in their stories. The
unintrusive narrator limits himself or herself to presenting the
story in an impartial and neutral manner. The observer perspective in recounting personal events may be conceived as
analogous to the unintrusive mode of narration. Conversely,
stories of memories from a field perspective, from one's own
point of view, may be perceived as intrusive narration.

Most of the episodes recounted by the retired teachers
were field memories told from the point of view of an intrusive
narrator who is involved and voices opinions and feelings concerning events and persons. The focus of many stories is on the
feelings and attitudes of the teachers who tend to tell their
story from their own point of view. Their high level of emotional
involvement expresses itself in their choice of terms and rhetorical devices. Sometimes emotions are referred to explicitly.

For instance:

>I had a feeling of elation. (Event no. 22)

>I was extremely moved. (Event no. 52)

>I was mortally afraid. (Event no. 65)

>I felt lost. (Event no. 68)

>I was left with a bad conscience. (Event no. 95)

Sometimes the personal point of view is presented through the use of *quantifiers*, intensifying a clause. For instance:

>*Everyone* thought like that. (Event no. 17)

>*We all* sinned by treating retarded children in a negative way. (Event no. 113)

>Many teachers used positive or negative adjectives when relating to the characters in their stories. For instance:

>A good student. (Event no. 67)

>A frightening woman. (Event no. 28)

>An able administrator. (Event no. 74)

>Problematic children. (Event no. 31)

Superlatives are another device reflecting emotional involvement from a personal point of view:

>An outstanding student. (Event no. 93)

>The most beautiful party. (Event no. 40)

>Unusually devoted. (Event no. 72)

>A wonderful lesson. (Event no. 114)

The school climate was outstanding. (Event no. 74)

Repetitions can create an affective tone. For instance:

The school climate was not good, it was not a warm climate. (Event no. 76)

I invested a lot of effort in this student, I invested so much in him. (Event no. 84)

The prevalent direct speech in the stories reflects the field perspective of the memories. For instance:

The mother shouted at me: "You are not a responsible person, you are behaving in an irregular manner." I answered: "I do not allow you to raise your voice in the kindergarten." (Event no. 12)

The father said: "My son will not do his homework." I answered: "Your son will take a pencil and paper to his friend and will prepare his homework there." (Event no. 57)

It is no wonder that the stories of teachers' memories reflect a high level of emotional involvement. The question arises, can they really remember their past attitudes?

Goethals and Reckman (1982) claim that people often cannot remember what they used to believe. Their study showed that after some attitude change had taken place, respondents tended to report their new attitudes when asked what attitude they had indicated at first. Recall seems to correlate better with present than with original opinion. It may well be that teachers' memories reflect their present attitudes more than their past convictions.

Barclay (1986) argues that "the person's current self-knowledge and feelings about self mediate the reconstructive process. In this sense autobiography is an artifact, not based in precise recollections but manufactures to best represent one's contemporary view of self" (p. 84).

Learning from experience means changing one's belief system, as well as constructing a set of practical rules and principles. Sometimes this change is commented on quite explicitly by the narrator. In Hannah's stories, for instance, the changes in attitudes are noted and explained in their relation to classroom experiences.

Goethals and Reckman (1982) suggest that "it is the act of changing our attitudes that we remember rather than attitudes themselves" (p. 179). In the professional events recalled by teachers, the phrases *since then* and *following that experience* reappear often, indicating that a change of attitude might be a powerful element in determining the outcome of the retrieval process. Still, the detailed and vivid stories of teachers convince us that they portray meaningful elements in their professional lives.

STYLISTIC ELEMENTS

Several stylistic elements are noted.

Use of Language

Teachers used mostly standard language in their stories, sometimes introducing common terms, especially when describing interpersonal relations. Examples of such expressions are:

> I had a serious "takel" with parents. [*Takel* is an expression for confrontation.] (Event no. 12)

> We made sulha. [*Sulha* is an expression for peacemaking.] (Event no. 29)

Metaphors appear only seldom and are mostly everyday expressions. For example:

> I did not lick honey [meaning "I did not have an easy time"]. (Event no. 67)

> It was difficult to put the class back on the tracks. (Event no. 126)

The Use of Professional-Theoretical Terms in Teachers' Memories

An important issue concerns the nature of teachers' professional knowledge as it is expressed in the use of theoretical terms by the retired teachers. Researchers of teaching have found that it is extremely difficult to capture the essence of craft knowledge. Leinhardt (1990) states that the "awareness of the value of the craft of practice has been accompanied by a realization that explicating the knowledge of craft has some inherent problems" (p. 19).

One of these inherent difficulties is that teachers do not tend to pass on their craft in an explicit way. Jackson (1968), for instance, found that teachers rarely use professional terms when talking about their craft. Jackson (1968) states that "one of the most notable features of teacher talk is the absence of technical vocabulary. Unlike professional encounters between doctors, lawyers, garage mechanics and astrophysicists when teacher talk together almost any reasonably intelligent adult can listen and comprehend what is being said. Occasionally familiar words are used in a specialized sense" (p. 143). Only a few professional terms were found in the memories of retired teachers. Here are some examples:

> I taught reading according to the global method. (Event no. 110)

> I used group teaching methods. (Event no. 133)

> I used project work. (Event no. 73)

> One of my student-teachers gave a lesson based on discovery learning. (Event no. 129)

The lack of use of professional terms originating in educational theory may be due to the fact that the participating teachers tried to share their recollected experiences, and appeared not to be interested in "showing off" their professional-theoretical knowledge. Telling your past personal story about teaching is not to be equated with lecturing about your practice.

SUMMARY COMMENTS

The stories of teacher memories were analyzed and discussed from three perspectives: the rhetorical macrostructure of the text, the point of view reflected in the story, and the stylistic characteristics of the text, especially the use of professional terms.

Coherence of the stories was examined according to various organizing principles: chronological connections, causal connections, contrastive connections, descriptive structures, deductive structures, and associative structures. Different beginnings and endings of stories were presented and interpreted.

Regarding points of view, a distinction was made between the perspective of an observer and one's own "field perspective." The lack of use of professional terms in the recalled events was noted.

The main autobiographical mode adopted by most teachers in the study was the oratory form. According to Barclay (1986), following Howarth (1980), "in oratory the autobiographer attempts to present an 'idealized self,' thereby offering an ideological message assumed to have significance for the reader" (Barclay 1986, p. 84).

The participating teachers apparently felt very strongly about their professional ideological messages. Sometimes these messages concern practical rules and principles, as in Hannah's case. Often the message concerns the hardships of teaching in extremely difficult circumstances, and the importance of adhering to one's commitment, thus overcoming all difficulties. It is significant and interesting that, overall, the teachers' stories conveyed an optimistic view of teaching, portraying their profession as providing opportunities for student growth and development. This tendency was discussed in chapter 5.

7

Experience, Professional Knowledge, and Memory of Events

> The word memory has a double meaning. Memory recalls past events, images and feelings, it also constitutes a challenge and a warning for the future.
> Rabin 1975, p. 8

🐾 HOW do teachers learn from past experience and transform their experience into professional knowledge? Clandinin and Connelly (1991) claim that the word *experience,* though universal in education, is mostly used with no special meaning and "functions as the ultimate explanatory context: 'Why do teachers, students and others do what they do? Because of their experience'" (p. 260). What is the role of experience in teaching and learning? How do teachers develop the ability to transform their knowledge about subject matter and pedagogy into teaching acts? And, not least intriguing, how is teachers' experience in schools transformed into professional knowledge, into the wisdom of practice (Shulman 1986)?

These are some of the questions that will be dealt with in this and following chapters. First, let us turn to some conceptual issues concerning the relationship between educational experience and the growth of professional knowledge about teaching.

STRUCTURES OF PRACTICAL KNOWLEDGE ABOUT TEACHING

One way of structuring the professional knowledge base of teaching was suggested by Elbaz (1981). To characterize the structure of practical knowledge of teachers, Elbaz chose terms that reflected the relationship between teachers' experience and some personal dimensions. These terms are *rule of practice, practical principles,* and *images.* According to Elbaz, rules of practice are "brief and clearly formulated statements of what to do or how to do it in a particular situation frequently encountered in practice" (p. 61).

Practical principles are more-inclusive statements than rules, embodying a rationale "that emerges at the end of a process of deliberation on a problem" (p. 61). Gauthier (1963) emphasizes the role of experience in constructing practical principles. In Gauthier's (1963) words, "Practical principles have been formulated as general practical judgments and serve to bring past experiences to bear on present problems" (p. 156).

Images are the most-inclusive structures of practical knowledge, according to Elbaz. These are "brief metaphorical statements of how teaching should be" (Elbaz 1981, p. 61), based on the teachers' past experience, theoretical knowledge, and personal beliefs. The study of teachers' memories reveals some of the rules of practice and practical principles of teachers, linked to their past experiences and based on their hard-won insights.

FORMS OF TEACHERS' KNOWLEDGE

Rules of practice and practical principles are important components of teachers' knowledge. What is the structure and form of this knowledge?

Shulman (1986) distinguishes three forms of teachers' knowledge: propositional knowledge, case knowledge, and strategic knowledge. According to Shulman, both the research-based principles of teaching and the experience-based recommendations imparted to teachers are posed as sets of propositions. Shulman argues that there are three types of propositional knowledge in the teaching domain: principles, maxims, and norms. Principles are derived from research, whether empirical or philosophical. An example of a research-originating principle is that teachers' wait-time between posing a question to one student and moving on to another one, or providing an answer, should be extended (Rowe 1974). Maxims are derived from practical experience and represent the individual or collective wisdom of practice. A teacher stating that she always keeps silent until her class quiets down is referring to such a maxim. A third kind of propositions reflects norms, values, and ideological commitments—for instance, the normative proposition that students have to be treated with consideration and fairness.

Though Shulman recognizes the power of principles as central components of teachers' knowledge, he claims that it is difficult to apply them in the particular circumstances of specific classrooms. He argues for the usefulness of case knowledge, saying that as a necessary "complement to propositional knowledge, case knowledge is knowledge of specific, well documented, and richly developed events" (Shulman 1986, p. 11).

The cases themselves may be perceived as pertaining to different types of knowledge: prototypes that exemplify theoretical principles; precedents that are embodiments of maxims and rules of practice that might govern the further actions of teachers. "These remembrances of teaching past are valuable in guiding the work of a teacher, both as a source for specific ideas and as a heuristic to stimulate new thinking" (Shulman 1986, p. 12).

Another form of case is the parable, which conveys norms and values. Any given case can serve more than one function—for instance, as both precedent and parable.

The following recalled event serves as an example:

> I started my work as a teacher in a small village in Lower Gallilea. As the only teacher I struggled with difficulties, problems, and doubts, all by myself. Due to these conditions I got to know my students very well. And yet there were incidents through which I became more aware of the characteristics of this or another child. I'll tell about one such case: Elizabeth was a big girl, generally unkempt, with a hole in her blouse, and messy books and copybooks. She was below average in her studies, not concentrated, sort of tired looking. One may say that she was not the teacher's pet nor a central figure in the class. And suddenly, on our first field trip to the hills, on an extremely hot and dry day, I discovered an Elizabeth I had not expected at all. All the children had finished drinking the water they had brought with them. Elizabeth passed her own bottle of water from one child to

another, admonishing them: "Don't drink too much, leave some water for Dan, for Gideon." We jump from rock to rock. At every steep corner Elizabeth pauses and stretches her hands out to whoever has difficulties or is afraid to jump. We returned home. I did not forget what I had seen. I started to encourage her and to remind the class of her actions during our field trip. Her self-image and achievements improved greatly. I am still in contact with her. She is a grandmother now and works as a nurse in her village, admired by everyone. How can one forget?

Event no. 106
Female elementary school teacher
Middle-class population
Years of practice at the time of the event: 1
Overall years of teaching: 30
Years since retirement: 10

This case may be conceived of as serving the function of precedent for the teacher, and as an embodiment of an implicit maxim: "Never judge students by their outward features." The case serves also as a parable, conveying norms and values of helping others. The ending may be understood to convey the message of the importance of the helping professions and of the centrality of memories of good deeds: "How can one forget?"

Deriving insights into one's past experiences is highly complex and can be problematic. Such situations may require what Shulman (1986) defines as strategic knowledge, which is necessary "when the lesson of single principles contradict one another, or the precedents of particular cases are incompatible" (p. 13).

A teacher's strategic knowledge is exemplified in the following event:

I had a student in kindergarten called Nava, who had a bad limp. She was very intelligent and capable. At the end of the year I gave her the main part in a play. Nava's mother approached me and complained that because of the performance everyone will become aware of Nava's limp. After a long conversation the mother accepted my decision. I told her: "Don't make the child feel inferior, let her express her abilities." The girl grew and at the end of her elementary school studies she performed the main part in the graduation play. I sat beside her mother, and both of us cried throughout the performance. Nava had grown, was very successful, and ready to appear in a main part in spite of her limp.

Event no. 37
Female kindergarten teacher
Heterogeneous population
Years of practice at the time of the event: 5
Overall years of teaching: 25
Years since retirement: 5

In this case the teacher needed strategic knowledge. Contradictory principles could have been applied in this situation: to shield the child from embarrassment, and to strengthen her ability to overcome her limitations. The teacher could have yielded to the mother's request, out of consideration and respect for a parent, she could stay firm in her decision and try to gain the mother's trust. The teacher used her strategic knowledge in making her choice and in carrying it through.

The remembered events of retired teachers communicate and integrate different messages, fulfilling the functions of prototypes, precedents, and parables. Shulman argues that the organization of cases in the form of stories, using the grammar of narrative forms of discourse, makes them readily stored and available in order to reflect on and gain understanding of past experiences as guides for further actions. Reflection is defined by Shulman as follows: "This is what a teacher does when he or she looks back at the teaching and learning that has occurred, and reconstructs, reenacts, and/or recaptures the events, the emotions, and the accomplishments. It is that set of processes through which a professional learns from experiences. It can be done alone or in concert, with the help of recording devices or solely through memory" (Shulman 1987, p. 19). The remembered events of teachers are the expressions of such reflection. This is the significant difference between memory of everyday life events, as reported in other studies, and the professional events in the lives of teachers. Whereas in the first context the recording of a remembered event, in introspective or experimental situations, does not necessarily involve the kind of reflection characterized by Shulman, recalling professional teaching events entails looking back at one's own teaching, one's personal past experiences and accomplishments, recapturing significant events, in order to derive some pedagogical insights.

PROFESSIONAL SOCIALIZATION AND THE ROLE OF EXPERIENCE

A brief look at another profession will provide some insights into the relationship between teachers' knowledge and their past experiences—from the point of view of professional socialization. Light, in his book *Becoming Psychiatrists: The Professional Transformation of Self* (1980), discusses the nature of professional socialization and the process of training for uncertainty and control. The kinds of uncertainty that Light refers to concern one's sense of imperfect mastery of available knowledge, the limitations of the existing knowledge base in the profession, and the lack of ability to distinguish between imperfect mastery of knowledge and imperfections in the knowledge itself. The process of learning to teach and practicing teaching share these basic uncertainties with psychiatry, and with various other professions.

Light argues that practitioners need, as well, to develop a sense of control. "Technically, a profession's greatest need is for a better expertise in the form of knowledge and skills, but sociologically, a profession's greatest need is for control. Thus a major, implicit goal of training in psychiatry and in other professions is to learn how to control the uncertainties of the situation at hand" (p. 282).

Light goes on to claim "that experience alone is considered to bring with it greater command over uncertainties which technical knowledge cannot provide" (p. 286). Technical knowledge does not "work" in all situations of practice. The deference to experience guarantees one's growing authority through establishing a repertoire of past success stories: "Residents gain a sense of mastery by collecting success stories which show them that they are effective and by selectively drawing on their growing number of cases to make clinical judgment" (p. 286).

Experience is perceived as leading to one's own selective definition of principles of practice. Once a trainee gains a personal sense of mastery over practical principles, there arises the danger of these becoming self-validating, diminishing one's responsiveness to the evaluation and criticism of others. This phenomenon may be even more dominant in a profession like teaching, which lacks the ongoing feedback provided in the hospital culture.

According to Light (1980): "A major way in which professionals learn how to control the uncertainties of treatment lies in the subtle shift from considering technique as a means to considering it an end. . . . The emphasis on technique in training for control, also leads the young professional to redefine what is competence. It eliminates the layman's definition of competence—whether the patient gets better—and redefines it in terms of clinical procedures" (p. 287). Learning from experience, in psychiatry as well as in teaching, can lead to this redefinition of competence, that doing the "right" thing is more important than the results.

Another characteristic of the growth of the practical knowledge of individual practitioners, as analyzed by Light, concerns the development of a personal clinical philosophy. "Psychiatric residents resolve difficulties of self-evaluation by incorporating an 'approach,' which then allows them to believe in themselves. Thus being comfortable and being effective become synonymous" (p. 294). Teachers, as well, are encouraged to develop their own educational philosophy in the face of the enormous uncertainties of their field of practice. Consequently, they might tend to acquire immunity to criticism. This tendency is sometimes expressed in the memories of retired teachers. A kindergarten teacher's anger at her supervisor can be explained this way. For instance, in Event no. 28 (see chapter 2) the teacher had managed to gain control over the uncertainties of her teaching situations through the development of her own way of acting. It was difficult for her to accept criticism from a supervisor whom she perceived as not knowing "what works" under specific conditions, especially if this criticism was voiced in harsh tones.

The process of professional socialization, according to this view, entails adherence to the notion that personalized rules of practice are desirable outcomes of learning from experience. Such hard-won expertise allows teachers to maintain control over the inherent uncertainties of their profession. The three-fold uncertainties mentioned by Light (1980)—namely, limitations of the existing base of professional knowledge, imperfect mastery of this knowledge, and the difficulties of distinguishing between those uncertainties—strengthen teachers' reliance on experiential knowledge embodied in memories of events.

It has been stated above that experience stored in the form of remembered events serves as a framework for understanding situations, and for acting upon this understanding. But what is the relationship between event knowledge and cognitive functioning?

EVENT KNOWLEDGE AND COGNITIVE FUNCTIONING

The relationship between event knowledge gained through experience and cognitive functioning has been examined by Nelson (1986), who concentrated on event knowledge and children's cognitive development. Nelson states that "what children represent of an experience has important implications for the possible abstract cognitive organization based on that experience" (p. 6). Nelson explored the ways in which children, and people in general, "impose structure on their experience to produce flexible, functional representations" (p. 7).

Nelson claims that perceptual representation is the most basic stage, and that other layers of representation may be conceived as a dynamic system in which different types of information are embodied in different structures. This dynamic view is shared as well by Schank (1982). Where Schank elaborates the notion of scripts (Schank and Abelson 1977), Nelson (Nelson and Gruendel 1981) talks about general event representations (GERs). GERs are conceived as very concrete representations incorporating temporal and spatial specifications. They are schemas in the sense that they organize data configurationally. According to Mandler (1979), a schema is "a spatially and/or temporally organized cognitive structure in which the parts are connected on the basis of contiguities that have been experienced in time or space. A schema is formed on the basis of past experience with objects, scenes, or events, and consists of (usually unconscious) expectations about what things look like and 'what goes with what' (p. 263).

According to Nelson (1986) GERs stand between primary perceptual representations and the more abstract layer of categorical knowledge. Lucariello and Rifkin (1986) conceived event representations as the basis for categorical knowledge. Their major premise is that "event representations constitute knowledge of experience in the world and that cognitive processes operate on these (and presumably other representations) rather than on the perceived world. Such operations, in turn, may lead to the construction of new forms of knowledge" (p. 189).

Two types of knowledge organization are suggested by Lucariello and Rifkin (1986): (1) hierarchically arranged taxonomic knowledge of object categories, identified with semantic memory, and (2) the event schema described above, a schematically organized memory system. These two types of knowledge organization are considered to be complementary and related.

Lucariello and Rifkin (1986) discuss the "slot filler" model for constructing taxonomic, hierarchical knowledge from the organized event schemas. Slot fillers are appropriate objects that accompany actions in event structures, such as "having lunch." Different kinds of food may occupy these slots over different occurrences of the event. Slot-filler categories are abstracted from alternative fillers of the slot and are formed on the basis of a shared function. Slot fillers are considered to form children's initial semantic category structure. Eventually event-representation-based categories develop into larger taxonomic categories, as slot-filler categories combine to form hierarchically organized taxonomic structures. Some of the processes involved in the formation of more-abstract mental representations may be categorization of similar elements, linear ordering, or organization into higher-level events.

It may well be that the development of organized taxonomic structures of teachers' professional knowledge is formed in an analogous model. For instance, novice teachers may experience different slot fillers within an organized structure, such as "starting a lesson," over different occasions of the event. On one occasion test sheets might be handed out by the teacher, while on another occasion the students might be asked to take out their books. The "starting a lesson" action can thus be accompanied by highly different objects, sharing the function of starting students' work in class.

The dynamically evolving script for teaching a lesson serves as the basis for deriving concept categories, in this case the category "instructional materials to be used in starting a lesson." The construction of such more-stable semantic structures might be one of the reasons teachers can find it difficult to introduce innovations into their modes of instruction. The formation of teachers' own concept categories, derived from past experiences over time, may yield fairly stable taxonomic structures that are not easily changed. Support for this view is provided by Nelson's (1986) observation that young children appear to form implicit rules of behavior for themselves and others, derived from their analysis of "the way things are," equating "the way it is" with "the way it should be." We find children insisting on certain routines in their everyday activities, such as the process of story reading before bedtime. In learning about their profession, teachers may find themselves in a similar role and position when learning about their world, a situation that can cause a certain rigidness concerning developed routines.

It is important to note, though, that the process described here does not preclude imaginative thought and conceptual innovation. As Nelson (1986) claims: "It is probable that all types of representations—specific memories, general schemas, abstract concepts—may be used within the cognitive system in the manipulation and transformation of old knowledge to produce novel constructions, such as plans, predictions, and imaginative thought" (p. 9).

Nelson (1986) discusses levels of representation in terms of explicit and implicit knowledge. The development of scripts for everyday events, whether in one's private life or in a professional context, may involve the transition from explicit to implicit knowledge. Thus a teacher may form a "lesson" script that consists of a series of brief terms, such as *starting a lesson,* representing formerly explicitly stated detached components of the ordered sequence of actions in their specific spatial and temporal context.

KNOWLEDGE ORGANIZATION AND ACCESS TO INFORMATION

Having discussed the nature of event knowledge and its transformation into taxonomic (i.e., semantic) knowledge, the question arises: How is knowledge organized and stored in memory, and what are the methods of accessing this information?

Researchers of memory for events have suggested various organizational structures holding relevant knowledge, such as scripts, generalized event representations (GERs), and memory organization packets (MOPs), some of which were discussed in previous chapters.

In the taxonomic organization of categories, category relationships are expressed in terms of class inclusion. Higher categories are more inclusive. For an example in the case of object categories, consider the categories "plants" and "fruit trees." The category "plants" is higher level and includes other categories besides "fruit trees." Basic levels of taxonomies can be identified at which objects share a significant number of attributes. It is unclear whether events can also be classified in terms of taxonomic levels, because events bear part-whole relations to each other, not class-inclusion relations; for instance, "set the table" is part of the "getting dinner ready" event. On the other hand, there is empirical evidence for adults' taxonomic organization of events based on class-inclusion relations (Cantor, Mischel, and Schwartz 1982).

A distinction has been made between physical and nonphysical features of events (Cantor, Mischel, and Schwartz 1982). Physical characteristics might concern persons, situations, and objects. Nonphysical features include personality traits, feelings, and atmosphere. Features of events can be placed along the concrete-to-abstract dimension, so it might be assumed that initial representations of events do not include much abstract information, which becomes more pronounced as representations become more elaborate with experience. Remembered events may constitute a reconstruction of the movement from a concrete description of classrooms and students to a more abstract level of feelings and attitudes. The story about Isri, as told by Hannah (Event no. 7), is an example of such a reconstruction, referring to both physical and nonphysical features of the reported event.

To sum up, event categories are formed through cognitive analysis, yielding higher-order knowledge. This knowledge can be accessed during everyday, as well as professional, planning and decision making. The following section describes a mode of professional planning and decision making, based on prior event knowledge that is reorganized and reframed in order to solve "puzzles of practice."

REFRAMING

Russell and Munby (1991) have studied the relationship between experience and the development of professional knowledge. Their goal was "to open up the process of learning by and from experience as well as to show the force of the construct of reframing in that process" (p. 165). In their analysis of two cases of experienced teachers facing "puzzles of practice," they discuss the nature of reframing taking place in diverse educational situations. In each case the teacher was confronted with a puzzle, such as how to establish classroom routines which work, or how to handle parental involvement. Through reframing their own grasp of the problem, through learning to see the situation in a new and different way, the teachers were able to handle their problems and extend their professional knowledge. In one case the teacher reframed the problem of class routines. Instead of perceiving it as a "management problem," she started to "see" it as a "learning problem." On the basis of this reframing, the teacher was able to invoke what she knew about learning at that age—in particular, that it requires practice, time, and patience. What she learned from this experience became part of her professional knowledge base.

An important element in the process of reframing a problem is sensitivity and attentiveness to "backtalk" from events in the classroom. One teacher described "how listening to the backtalk from events in his classroom alters his view of learning and consequently his approach to teaching" (p. 175).

Three concepts—puzzles of practice, backtalk, and reframing—may be viewed as key to understanding how experience is transformed into professional knowledge. The dynamic nature of professional events can be related to the interplay of these concepts. A professional script may prove to be unsatisfactory for a teacher, generating a puzzle of practice. Through attentiveness to the backtalk of the situation, whether expressed in students' words and behavior or in other kinds of messages, the teacher can respond by reframing the problem, thus creating a new script.

THE SOCIAL-HISTORICAL CONTEXT OF
TEACHERS' KNOWLEDGE

The development of professional knowledge is not a solitary activity. Teachers have emphasized the crucial role of interpersonal relations in their professional lives. The impact of historical and environmental context on their knowledge is reflected in their stories. Bruner (1990) argues that coming to know anything is a process that is both situated in a cultural context and distributed as part of a social knowledge flow of which one has become a part. "To overlook this situated—distributed nature of knowledge and knowing is to lose sight not only of the cultural nature of knowledge but of the correspondingly cultural nature of knowledge acquisition" (p. 106).

Britzman (1986) claims that "student teachers need to understand how the interaction between time, place, people, ideas, and personal growth contributes to the process of professional development" (p. 442–43). Britzman's analysis of the processes involved in making a teacher (i.e., developing professional knowledge) closely resembles Light's analysis of the making of psychiatrists. In both cases practitioners face uncertainty concerning the body of knowledge that is at their disposal. Britzman says that "the fear most commonly articulated by prospective teachers is that they will never know enough to teach. Behind this fear is the larger cultural expectation that teachers must be certain in their knowledge" (p. 450).

Both views emphasize control. Britzman refers to the equating of learning with control. Especially significant in Britzman's view is the notion, or the "cultural myth," that teachers are self-made and form their own professional identity—an identity that is self-validating—and that teachers never need to change, or even explain their professional actions. "Thus the myth that teachers are self-made serves to cloak their social relationships and the context of school structure by exaggerating personal autonomy" (Britzman 1986, p. 452).

Britzman proposes that "disequilibrium" is a necessary condition for the transformation from being a former student to the status of being a teacher. Disequilibrium is a process "of making of, and acting within, self-doubt, uncertainty, and the unexpected, while assuming a role which requires confidence, certainty and stability" (p. 452). In terms of memory research this is a process of establishing new ways of seeing classroom events, of continuous reframing and creating new, ever-flexible scripts (Schank 1982). In the memories of teachers we have found evidence of disequilibrium, leading to new knowledge.

SUMMARY COMMENTS

Different concepts about the relationship between experience and professional knowledge were presented in this chapter. The structures of practical knowledge of teaching were discussed and exemplified by the recalled events of retired teachers. Professional socialization and the role of experience in becoming professionals were discussed, comparing teaching with other professions. Ways of linking event knowledge and organized taxonomic knowledge were presented. Reframing was discussed as a possible mode for developing professional knowledge. Finally, the social-historical context of teachers' knowledge was emphasized.

In the next chapter we shall follow teachers' own accounts of the importance of interaction in the process of their professional development, transforming experience into knowledge.

8

Learning from Experience:
The Teachers' View

The amount of expertise varies in inverse proportion
to the number of statements understood by the
general public.
Gummidge's Law (Dickson 1978, p. 76)

🐾 THIS chapter focuses on retired teachers' views concerning the relationship between experience and knowledge. After looking at some statements of retired teachers, we'll discuss the main themes of teachers' views about the transformation of experiences into professional wisdom.

TEACHERS' VIEWS ABOUT LEARNING
FROM EXPERIENCE

Let us listen to some of the retired teachers' responses to the following questions: How does professional knowledge develop? What is the role of experience in this process?

- "There are different types of teachers. I remember events concerning learning materials. Rules and principles develop later but they originate in early experiences."
- "Experience comes first. People learn from their experience, especially from problems and failures. My own failure at learning math helped me devise alternative ways of teaching math."
- "Our successes, achievements, and positive results are the basis for transforming experience into knowledge. A class discussion after a successful

131

lesson, or the results of a test, teach me how to teach."

- "Successes or failures, or some sudden insight, are important factors in reaching conclusions about teaching. I remember that parents used to forget the grade level of their children. We used to make fun of them. And then a similar event happened to me. My son forgot his lunch box at home. On my way I met two students from his school. I asked them to give him his lunch box, but I could not remember in which grade he was, seventh or eighth. I was extremely ashamed. Many families used to have large numbers of children, and I had only three. And yet one can forget. My conclusion was that being compassionate was the most important quality of a teacher."

- "Learning from experience is a process and takes time. One has to experience failures. In my literature lessons I once reprimanded three students for not relying on their own knowledge when analyzing a novel by Camus: *The Pest.* It turned out that their previous teacher had insisted on using scholarly sources. I learned from this event that one has to encourage students to trust themselves and their ability to understand a literary text. How do you do this? By helping them to participate in the lesson and to think for themselves. This event was a turning point for me. It is not enough to think about instructional strategies; teacher and students have to be explicitly conscious of the teaching-learning approach. I used certain techniques, such as noting titles and captions on the blackboard, in order to stimulate the creative thinking of my students."

These statements highlight the importance of learning from one's failures and successes. It may well be that unusual instances of positive or negative professional experiences are imprinted in memory and may be recalled as guides for further actions.

Some teachers express the need to link any rule of practice to a concrete event:

- "There is a connection between principles and events. I personally require concrete evidence for any generalization."
- "Whenever I mentioned a certain rule, I thought about the event connected to it."

Other teachers emphasized the cooperative and interpersonal aspects of learning from experience.

- "In my work as a cooperative teacher I used to tell my student-teachers the stories I shared with you. I asked them to analyze these events with me—in this manner we reached some general conclusions."
- "The sources of many principles of accountability and commitment are to be found in one's home. Rules live and survive through discussion, otherwise they are lost. It is not enough to act on the basis of certain principles, debating and examining them is very important. One may reflect on these principles in solitude, but I need interaction with others."
- "The intensity of interpersonal relationships determines our learning from experience. Sometimes I wish to identify with a person, sometimes I have a sudden insight, sometimes I get positive reinforcement from the environment. All these are channels for learning from experience. Whenever I learn a rule or principle I continue to discover new insights which depend on the environment in which I work."

These statements emphasize the role of interpersonal relations and the importance of sharing one's experiences with colleagues.

THEMES OF LEARNING FROM EXPERIENCE

The retired teachers in our study had different views about the significance of various factors in the process of transforming experience into professional rules and principles. Many mentioned the *close connection between experience and rules of practice.* This view seems to be congruent with Connelly and Clandinin's (1985, 1986) approach to personal practical knowledge. Stories of practice come to constitute a narrative unity that reflects teachers' past experiences. Experiential elements are conceived as being "on call" for when the appropriate situations arise. One teacher in our study put it this way: "Teacher seniority is very important. As experience accumulates, particular and specific events turn into rules."

It is important to note that the distinction between rule and experience can be imposed by the research question itself, whereas teachers might not "codify" their professional knowledge in terms of rules and principles in their daily practice, except in situations that require such codification. In some situations, such as in the teachers' lounge, teachers may discuss classroom events, seeking advice or sharing insights. In such circumstances teachers might tend to pronounce their rules of practice. In their regular work context, teachers might use explicit rules and principles in the 'preactive' phase of teaching, while planning their lessons. Involvement in teacher education programs as cooperative teachers creates another situation for sharing codified practical knowledge with student-teachers. Educational research in its many forms sets the stage for statements concerning teachers' personal practical knowledge. Yet even in these situations the sharing of knowledge may depend to a large extent on the narrative form, linking knowledge to past experience.

The Narrative Mode of Thought

Bruner (1986) characterizes the narrative mode as being distinct from the paradigmatic mode, which is a formal system of description and explanation. Says Bruner: "The imaginative application of the narrative mode leads instead to good stories, gripping drama, believable (though not necessarily 'true') historical accounts. It deals in human or human-like intention and action and the viccisitudes and consequences that mark their course. It strives to put its timeless miracles into the particulars of experience, and to locate the experience in time and place" (p. 13). Stories have a structure. In Bruner's words: "What gives the story its unity is the manner in which plight, characters, and consciousness interact to yield a structure that has a start, a development, and 'a sense of an ending' " (p. 21). We have seen above how the recollected memories of retired teachers exhibit the features of stories, as defined by Bruner (1986).

A most interesting point made by Bruner concerns the power of stories to guide action in different occupations—for instance, in economy. Bruner states: "There is a curious anomaly here: businessmen and bankers today (like men of affairs of all ages) guide their decisions by just such stories—even when a workable theory is available" (p. 42).

Bruner concludes that in the end the narrative and the paradigmatic come to lie side by side. We have seen this coexistence of two modes of thought reflected in the stories of retired teachers. A good example is the story told in great detail in Event no. 6 (see chapter 2) concerning the teaching of English grammar. The story ended as follows:

1. Every teacher, at every class level, has to view himself or herself as part of a chain.
2. It is very important for all teachers to study the structure of the discipline they teach.
3. Continuous involvement in curriculum development and change is part of the teaching profession. (Assuming that 70% to 80% of the curriculum is stable and does not change.)

These statements are general propositions that can be transformed into principled hypotheses.

The self as a storyteller (Bruner 1990, p. 111) is central to the notion of teachers as constructors of professional knowledge. Bruner claims that "people narrativize their experience of the world and their own role in it" (p. 115). This narrativized experience can then guide one's own further action, and can, as well, be shared with one's colleagues. Schubert (1992) presents findings from the Teacher Lore Project, a research project at the University of Illinois. When teachers were invited to share their knowledge about teaching, they often communicated their knowledge best through stories about their experiences.

The role of narrative in the personal practical knowledge of teachers has been treated in depth by Connelly and Clandinin (1985, 1986). Personal practical knowledge is defined as an account of how teachers know their teaching situations. In Connelly and Clandinin's (1985) words: "Personal practical knowledge is experienced, embodied and reconstructed out of the narratives of a user's life" (p. 183). These investigators emphasize the experiential understanding to be found in narrative accounts of field notes and interviews. These narrative accounts serve to unlock the "narrative units" of practitioners. "Narrative unity is a continuum within a person's experience which renders life experiences meaningful through the unity they achieve for the person. What we mean by unity is a union in a particular person in a particular time and place of all that has been and undergone in the past" (p. 198). What starts a story of practice, as reflected in field notes and interviews, culminates in a "narrative unity," expressing teachers' past experiences, personal histories, and cultural-historical context.

The study of retired teachers' memories is not based on observers' field notes or on interviews carried out over long period of time. Therefore, no attempt was made to construct narrative unity in the sense referred to by Connelly and Clandinin (1985). Still, the narrative mode of knowing teaching and learning situations is clearly reflected in the recalled events.

The statements of retired teachers constitute evidence for the strong and intimate linkage between concrete experience and professional knowledge. For instance: "Whenever I mentioned a certain rule, I thought about the event connected to it."

Jackson (1968) discusses the "intuitive, rather than rational approach to classroom events" and the "narrowness in the working definitions assigned to abstract terms" (p. 144). Jackson claims that the impulses and intuitive hunches of teachers "had been tempered by years of practical experience." Acknowledging the major role past experience plays in teachers' professional actions, Jackson offers an interesting explanation for the "here and nowness" of teachers' talk, which is reflected, as well, in the memories of retired teachers. Jackson argues that "the focus of the teacher's concern is on the concrete experience with a particular group of students . . . she lives in a world of *sharp existential boundaries*" (p. 147, emphasis in the original). "Moreover," Jackson states, "many of the unique features of her world become so well known to the teachers that it becomes difficult for her mentally to erase their identity and think of them as merely concrete manifestations of more abstract phenomena" (p. 147). It seems that retired teachers continue to live in the world of concrete existential boundaries.

Passage of Time

Some teachers thought that the passage of time was an important factor in learning from experience. "A time lag between an experience and professional rules is essential." The perception of a slow maturation process of personal practical knowledge was explained by the need for "emotional maturity and the ability to be critical of oneself," as one teacher stated.

The crucial role that maturity plays in the development of professional knowledge was noted by Sikes (1985). In her work on teachers' life cycles, Sikes found that in phase 3 (the thirty- to forty-year-old group), "the conjunction of experience and a relatively high level physical and intellectual ability mean that in terms of energy, involvement, ambition and self-confidence many teachers are at their peak" (p. 47–48). This is the period for consolidation of competence in one's chosen profession. According to Sikes (1985), in the next phase, at the forty- to fifty-five-year-old level, "adapting to 'maturity' can mean a new life structure, and new roles. By virtue of their seniority and age, within a school, teachers of forty plus are often authority figures" (p. 53). The retired teachers, who commented on the importance of maturity in the process of professional development, seem to echo the findings of Sikes. The importance of time and maturity in gaining professional wisdom raises interesting questions concerning the feasibility of sharing experiential knowledge with novice teachers. It might be unreasonable to expect that sharing the experience of mentor teachers with student teachers and novices through verbal communication fulfills the need for personalizing and constructing knowledge based on one's own experiences accumulated over time. Chapter 10 will deal with some implications of this for teacher education and school administration.

Disequilibrium and Reframing

Though the teachers didn't use terms like *disequilibrium* or *reframing,* their reflections on the growth of professional knowledge seem to imply such processes. Puzzles of practice (Russell and Munby 1991), whether unexplained failures or successes that were unaccounted for, created a disequilibrium in teachers' grasp of the situation.

The story of the teacher of literature presented above exemplifies this process. The inability of her "good" students to deal with a problem in understanding a novel constituted a puzzle that was solved after reframing it, not as weakness or lack of motivation in the students, but as stemming from previous learning experiences that called for a conscious relearning process.

It is contended herewith that the notions of disequilibrium and reframing are central for relating to one's own or others' experiences. Learning from experience does not necessarily mean that we continue to act in ways that proved to be successful in the past, or refrain from repeating unsuccessful actions. It may as well mean that we view our experience from new perspectives.

Collective Remembering

The emphasis put on learning from experience as a *socially constructed activity* by the participating teachers is striking. Again and again the teachers claimed that they need interaction with others in order to reflect on their experience and clarify some possible generalizations in the forms of rules and principles. This phenomenon may be understood in terms of collective remembering (Middleton and Edwards 1990b). The term *collective remembering* reflects "a shift from a predominant concern with individual memory, as process or content, to a direct consideration of remembering and forgetting as inherently social activities" (p. 1). The social nature of memory may express itself in the joint action of remembering together, as in acts of commemoration. Collective remembering is a distributed cognitive activity, when groups, in work and leisure contexts, reconstruct ways to achieve some common goals. In this sense collective remembering is very close to Bruner's (1990) conception of knowledge acquisition (quoted previously): "To overlook this situated-distributed nature of knowledge and knowing is to lose sight not only of the cultural nature of knowledge but of the correspondingly cultural nature of knowledge acquisition" (p. 106). The developing professional knowledge of teachers is dependent on interaction, as one of the retired teachers said: "It is not enough to act on the basis of certain principles, debating and examining them is very important."

In the collective-remembering approach the individual's memory is perceived not as being a passive storehouse of past experiences, but as changing through communicative processes in order to transform what is remembered in relation to present circumstances. Such reconstruction is highly meaningful in institutional contexts, which have a distinctive effect on remembering (Douglas 1986). Middleton and Edwards (1990b) claim that "in the contest between varying accounts of shared experiences, people reinterpret and discover features of the past that become the context and content for what they will jointly recall and commemorate on future occasions" (p. 7). According to their approach, "cognition itself and in particular remembering is achieved and represented in people's talk with each other" (p. 11). Middleton and Edwards emphasize the theme of knowledge sharing and using "as a form of collective memory in work settings" (p. 16). Of special interest to educators is Orr's (1990) analysis of a "community memory." According to Orr the most significant characteristic of working talk is its narrative structure. Orr states that "the stories in the community memory are produced in the real work of diagnosis and are further useful because their form prepares them for use in the next narrative creation of sense out of facts" (p. 186). In telling stories of how one has solved difficult problems, practitioners show themselves as being competent—and are being competent--through the preservation and circulation of knowledge. The narrative form of community memory is perceived as fulfilling another important function, namely, the construction of the professional identity of members of the community. Orr quotes Meyerhof (1986), who argued that "one of the most persistent but elusive ways that people make sense of themselves is to show themselves to themselves . . . by telling themselves stories. . . . More than merely self-recognition, self-definition is made possible by means of such showings, for their content may state not only what people think they are but what they should have been or may yet be" (Meyerhof 1986, p. 261).

The process of collective remembering is conceived herewith as crucial for the teaching profession, as teachers share their knowledge in the form of stories about past events. Teachers' lounges may be an ideal setting for such collective remembering to take place. The diagnosis and treatment of certain learning or behavior problems can proceed on the basis of discussing past events. Common knowledge concerning specific problems can be established and maintained within oral renarrations of past problems. The other aspect of collective remembering is not less important. "Although telling stories preserves potentially arcane and idiosyncratic pieces of information as part of the community of practice 'a community memory' it also serves to establish a continued identity of the teller as a competent practitioner, as a 'member of the community,' contributing to the 'community memory' of service practice" (Middleton and Edwards, 1990b, p. 17). As one's individual professional identity is shaped through collective remembering, so does this process serve to establish the ethos of schools. Telling "our" stories and discussing their implications for action creates a common way of doing things in "our" school. The process of collective remembering becomes a channel for the induction of novice teachers to the culture of schools.

A number of conclusions concerning the nature of learning from experience may be drawn from the above. Teachers claim that there exists a strong relationship between the remembered event and the rule of practice that originated from it. For some teachers the event becomes a rule and is recalled whenever appropriate circumstances arise. In these cases one might argue, according to Wyer and Scrull (1989), that when people are called upon to make a decision in their daily lives (e.g., in a classroom situation), an event schema can be retrieved that describes what typically occurs in such a situation and its likely consequences. The activated representation serves as a guide in inferring what sort of responses should be made. Wyer and Scrull claim that "the accessibility of event sequences . . . depends on the frequency and recency with which they have been formed and used in the past" (p. 252). The close connection between rules of action and recalled events is expressed in teachers' words like these: "I personally require concrete evidence for any generalization." The narrative form of events serves the creation of a community memory through continuous interpersonal sharing of experiences. It seems that "working talk" based on stories of one's own experiences is the basis for learning from experience. The teachers themselves are aware of this dependency and express it when discussing their own learning from experiences.

It is interesting to compare these findings with the findings of Alexander, Muir, and Chant (1992), who collected personal narratives of student-teachers who were asked to describe how they learned to teach. The student-teachers' views about learning to teach from their practicum were highly individualistically oriented, lacking the kind of emphasis on interaction with colleagues that was identified in the views of retired teachers. Obviously student-teachers were as yet unaware of the potential impact of this interaction on one's learning from experience.

It seems that the process of learning from experience changes throughout the professional life cycle of teachers. The main aspect of change is the growing role of interpersonal interaction with colleagues, and the creation of a professional community memory through collective remembering of past experiences.

SUMMARY COMMENTS

This chapter focused on teachers' views concerning the relationship between experience and professional knowledge. Statements of retired teachers were presented, and several emerging themes of learning from experience were discussed: the narrative mode of sharing knowledge, the close connection between experienced events and rules of practice, the maturation process of professional knowledge, reframing as serving the process of learning from experience, learning from experience as a socially constructed activity, and the notion of collective remembering.

9

Context-Specific Memories of Teachers and Learning from Experience: Some Conclusions

I remember how I would feel. I remember why I would like someone . . . or why I did not like a teacher. I think just remembering these things can give you a general idea of what you want to do, what you want to be and what you want your children to think of you.
(No. 67 F24-3d in Lortie 1975, p. 79)

RETIRED teachers' stories are conceived in this book as providing us with a glimpse of their professional identities, and with a view of the growth of their wisdom of practice. It is important to note that the analysis of teachers' memories, while focusing on the main themes of their stories, on their commonalities and differences, and on the manner in which concrete experiences are transformed into professional knowledge, does not entail any judgmental perspectives. Buchman (1992) warns us against taking sides and adopting partial views when considering teacher memories. Neither the "gloomy" view of the contents of teachers' minds as conservative, obstructing progress nor the "rosy" view of teachers' memories as illuminating and inspiring is acceptable. Buchman reminds us that "in research and scholarship, the question is not 'whose side you are on?' but 'what makes conceptual, empirical, and ethical sense?' " (p. 19). What sense can we make of the stories of teachers' memories?

Narrative knowledge, according to Bruner (1986) involves the construction of stories that give meaning to experience. The stories of teachers are "small stories" (Alexander, Muir, and Chant 1992) that emerge from personal perspectives and are located in the social-historical and cultural context in which they take place. No claim for generalizability is made, but the stories of retired teachers add to our understanding of the nature of teachers' professional memory and shed some light on the process of learning from experience, as well as on the intricacies of the practice of teaching.

RESULTS OF THE STUDY

What insights could be gained concerning teachers' memories of professional events?

Some basic findings and conclusions about memory of events in general have been validated regarding teachers' professional memories. The perceived importance of events, their emotionality, their level of surprise, and how often they have been rehearsed, determine their accessibility. Teachers' memories conform to the "reminiscence" phenomenon, and also to the notion that events that have primary functions in a person's life, especially in transition periods, have a high survival and retrieval rate.

The results of the present study deviate from some general findings in their relative emphasis on negative events. There might be a salient difference between teachers' professional memories, which tend to include negative incidents, and purely personal memories, which may tend to keep silent about negative events. The importance of negative events may be accounted for by their function as critical incidents in teachers' professional lives.

Another important aspect of teachers' memories of events is the tendency of teachers to tell stories of moral significance and to refer to the moral of their stories in the form of practical rules and principles, emanating from their recalled experiences. Hansen (1992) documents the emergence of a shared morality in a classroom. He claims that "to appreciate the symbolic and moral dimensions of what takes place in a classroom requires time and reflection, perhaps the mirror image of what a teacher and her students need to bring an environment into being in the first place" (p. 359). Retired teachers had the time and the opportunities to reflect upon the moral dimensions of their experiences, and are eager to share those with their audience. Teaching is a moral craft, and it is, therefore, no wonder that teachers' recalled events relate to isues of morality. The impact of context on the nature of recalled events is deemed to be a central finding of the present study. Context is treated not merely as background, or as a factor of social influence, but as the substance of memory itself.

Three environmental factors have been shown here to be an integral part of teachers' memories:

- The type of school in which teachers had taught (kindergarten or school)
- The historical period when the event occurred
- The socioeconomic level of the student population involved in the recalled event

The influence of context on teachers' memories of events is crucial for understanding their learning from experience and the situated nature of their knowledge. If memory of events is the basis for action in social and professional contexts, if memory defines our professional selves, then it is extremely important that memories of professional events be context specific, so that they can lead to defensible professional actions. Experiential memories (Cohen 1989) involve the reliving of experiences and are associated with images and feelings. Teachers who are able to relive their context-specific experiences might be better able to deal with classroom events in comparable situations. Moreover, because of the context-specific nature of their memories, teachers might be able to judge when their past experiences are not appropriate in fast-changing educational situations. "I teach the way I remember—only if my memory fits the context of my present teaching." On the other hand, the context-specific nature of teachers' professional memories can make teachers more resistant to change and adaptation, whenever they might be tempted to impose past insights and scripts on new classroom situations.

LEARNING FROM EXPERIENCE

Learning from experience does not need vindication. "Sharing professional experiences is such as essential element of professional growth that it has become axiomatic that in-service events should provide opportunities for participants to describe their experiences, reflect on the meanings of personal practice, and exchange interpretations with others" (Ross and Regan 1993). Ross and Regan state that in spite of the universal enthusiasm for this approach there have been few studies related to it. On the basis of their own study Ross and Regan conclude that interaction with narrators, who describe their professional experiences, had a positive effect on district consultants participating in an in-service program. In another in-service program for foreign-language teachers, it was shown how the shared professional discourse contributed to the complexity of the teachers' thinking about their teaching and helped the teachers gain greater control over their classroom practice (Freeman 1991)

In the present study, retired teachers claimed that sharing their experiences with colleagues, or with student-teachers, furthered the clarification and consolidation of their professional knowledge. Discussing one's experiences with others can be conceived as rehearsing professional events, thereby enhancing the survival and retrieval of their memories. Thus, shared discourse concerning one's past has a *synergetic effect* on the development of teachers' professional knowledge. Sharing one's experiences fosters insights and strengthens their survival in memory. Through remembering these experiences, teachers build a reservoir of professional knowledge, which in turn provides the basis for further sharing with colleagues. In this way the distributed character of knowledge is manifested. The process of sharing one's memories about past experiences can be conceived as representing a situation of *secondary functionality.* Survival of teachers' memories from the early part of their career has been explained on the basis of early events possessing functional primacy. It may well be that not only is shared discourse concerning one's experiences an opportunity for rehearsal, but, because of the importance teachers attach to them, those opportunities turn into secondary periods of primacy, enhancing the retrieval of discussed events.

A most important outcome of teachers' shared discourse is its impact on their sense of their professional identity and of their belonging to a well-defined professional culture with a common knowledge base.

Sharing of experiences can be conceived of as a process of collective remembering (Middleton and Edwards 1990a) through which "your memories and my memories" become part of a "community memory." Thus community memory constitutes part of the school culture that might be quite resistant to change and innovation (Sarason 1971). As professional uncertainty gives way to growing certainty, and as the need for control over one's practice is fulfilled (Light 1980), teachers may tend to cling to their beliefs and orientations, and might become more resistant to and wary of any critique. Teachers' voices in their recalled events have a ring of assurance and satisfaction. Most important, on the positive side, they are voices of optimism concerning the role of education and its contribution to the individual and to society. Many of the remembering teachers mentioned successes in very difficult situations. This general positive view of teaching was discussed in chapter 5. One teacher's words capture this feeling: "All beginnings are difficult, but it is possible to overcome all limitations and constraints."

10

Teachers' Memories:
Implications for Teacher Education
and School Administration

Ask any teacher or professor: 'How did you learn to
teach?' As likely as not, the response will be 'by teaching' or 'by experience', and little more will follow, as
though the answer were obvious and unproblematic
        Russell and Munby 1991, p. 164

🖋 THIS final chapter addresses some implications of this
study for teacher education and school administration. Different modes of using teachers' recollected stories and scripts are
discussed.

ANALYSIS OF TEACHERS' RECOLLECTIONS
OF EVENTS AND LESSON SCRIPTS

Teachers' stories about professional events represent cases of
practice, which can be analyzed and discussed in pre- and in-
service courses.

An example of such a discussion relates to the story of Isri
(Event no. 7), which concerns a case of a student getting hurt,
focusing on his, and his teacher's, reactions. The story ends
with a set of rules and principles derived from the incident. A
group of teachers, in an in-service course, analyzing and discussing this event were asked to focus on three issues: (1)
What is this a case of? (2) What similar incidents have they
experienced? (3) Could the "rules and principles" of the story be
useful in other cases, and if so, how?

Several themes emerged in the discussion that followed
the presentation of Isri's story. The teachers suggested that this

story was a case of (1) classroom safety, (2) teachers' reactions to unforeseen events, (3) students' interactions, (4) trauma in the classroom, and (5) construction of memory. The story evoked memories of similar incidents that were related by the participants with great animation and personal involvement. The clearly stated rules and principles, which are part of Isri's story, provided an opportunity to make possible distinctions between rules, such as the rule about hanging classroom posters, and principles, such as the principle that a student's reaction to pain is an indicator of her or his character. The nature of pain in classrooms was discussed, and diverse applications of the rules and principles of Isri's case were suggested.

Isri's story is a case of practice that takes us beyond the regular teaching situation in classrooms. It concerns additional parameters of teachers' roles during breaks and while confronting incidents of pain and confusion. Such incidents might not present themselves during everyday classroom observations, but they constitute a noteworthy part of the school culture and can be introduced in teachers' education programs through a case literature.

Cases that are based on the recollections of retired teachers fulfill an additional vital role in teacher education programs. They serve to create a sense of professional identity and continuity. The recalled events seem to bear this message: "We have been there before . . . . That is the way teaching is . . . . We did find solutions to many problems . . . .We did succeed!"

On the other hand, professional events of the past mark the differences between then and now, and may be useful in reflecting on some of the changes in the educational system and in society in general. Such changes might be ideological, such as the move toward heterogeneous classes and student integration. The changes might be expressed in different emphases in subject-matter domains, such as teaching science and technology in a societal context, or the introduction of bilingualism. Some changes might be conceived as "technical" such as the expanding functions of computers in schools, thought this change can have far-reaching educational consequences. Through careful analysis of teachers' stories of the past, it is possible to trace the roots of some of these changes and to discuss their implications for teachers today and tomorrow.

The "hidden curriculum" may be an interesting construct to use in the analysis of teachers' recollections. What role do socio-economic background and perceived intelligence play in teachers' plans and classroom activities? It might be easier for student-teachers, or for teachers in staff-development, to focus on these issues while looking at stories of long ago. At a next step their insights may be used for trying to understand present-day events. Moreover, the hidden curriculum of relationships between teachers and their colleagues, or supervisors, is seldom treated in teacher education programs. The recollection of retired teachers may provide ample examples of the power relations in schools.

THEMES FOR THE PRACTICUM

Several main themes have been identified as playing a role in the process of transforming experiences into the wisdom of practice. These themes may form the basis for reflecting on the practicum of teacher education programs. Some of the issues to be dealt with in teacher education programs are these:

- The role of failures. What does it mean to learn from one's mistakes?
- The role of successes. Under what circumstances could they be repeated?
- The intimate linkage between experienced events and rules of practice. What do we remember, the event or the rule? As practitioners, are we inclined to rely on the narrative mode of thought? What would this mean for our professional growth? How do we integrate theory and personal narrative?

These themes may play a major role in discussions between cooperating teachers, tutors, and mentors, and the student teachers or novice teachers they work with. Such issues may be deliberated before or after classroom observations, experiences, as well as during planning of, or reflection on, student teachers' own teaching episodes.

The notion of reframing is another useful theme for teacher education. Starting with instances of reframing in teachers' recollection, one can move to the elaboration of reframing in one's own practice.

Recollected events can function as part of a case literature in teacher education (Shulman 1992). Classroom observation can be guided by pertinent recollections of teachers which may be used for a close look at the evaluation and self-evaluation of teaching. Recollected events might pertain to the teaching of specific subject matter issues, or to certain pedagogical concerns. Thus it is possible to gain insights into one's own teaching of multiplication through careful analysis of past teaching events described by other math teachers teaching the same topic at the same grade level. On the other hand, student teachers or teachers in staff-development situations, might find it useful to reflect on recollections of teachers that concern issues of classroom management, or group work, in heterogenous classes.

Recollected events, functioning as part of a case literature in teacher education programs, are characterized by several features. These events have survived in the memory of their narrators, and may be perceived as representing essential elements of practice. The narrative structure of the events might provide conclusions, judgements, and resolution of dilemmas, offering fruitful avenues for case analysis and discussion. Simulation and role-play exercises can be based on recalled events, providing opportunities for analysis of, and reflection on, practice.

Student-teachers, and teachers participating in in-service programs, may be asked by their tutors to interview teachers about their past professional events in order to gain insights into the process of learning from experience and awareness of the role of memory in this process.

COLLECTIVE REMEMBERING AND TEACHER
COLLABORATION

Some Administrative Aspects

A critical lesson to be learned from the study of teachers' memories pertains to the importance of interpersonal relationships and the process of collective remembering. Sharing one's stories and reflecting jointly on the practice of teaching in teacher education and staff development settings can lay the ground for a more cooperative mode of teaching in schools. It is deemed essential that school administrators allocate a suitable place, as well as appropriate time, for collective remembering to take place. The sharing of one's experiences may focus on specific issues, like teaching a certain subject-matter component, such as photosynthesis. On the other hand, more-general educational issues may be discussed, such as the nature of homework or modes of student evaluation. The groups of teachers participating in these meetings could vary, according to topic and interest. These meetings do not have to be formal, with a chairperson and minutes taken. A pronounced formal character might indeed be counterproductive to the achievement of a growing shared knowledge base among teachers. Not only are events situated in context, but the telling about an incident is situated as well in a certain context. Therefore it is important to be aware of the contextual features of the situation in which collective remembering takes place. Who are the participants? What time slots are set aside for teachers' talk to go on undisturbed? Do teachers meet in a noisy teachers' lounge, or do they have other options of suitable locations? What is the institutional attitude toward teachers' "war stories"? Does the principal participate in some meetings? All of these are pertinent questions concerning the context of sharing one's stories, which can have consequences for the process of learning from experience. The emphasis on interpersonal relations in retired teachers' recollections itself highlights the human aspects of teaching.

Teacher collaboration is considered by researchers and educational reformers to be an essential feature of successful and innovative schools (Rosenholtz 1991; Fullan and Stiegelbauer 1991). Teachers' voices concerning the central role of interpersonal relations in their profession might be viewed as the basis for creating appropriate collaborative situations. Little (1990) argues for the importance of joint work as a prerequisite for truly collective action, based on shared responsibility for the practice of teaching. Joint work is dependent on administrative arrangements and on allocation of resources. Designing and setting up the necessary organizational structures is the role of school administrators. Little claims that "the greater the prospect for mutual influence among teachers, the more consequential becomes the substance of teachers' joint work; the beliefs teachers hold and their substantial knowledge of subject and student." (p. 523) It is contended herewith that settings of collective remembering of professional events in teacher education programs might set the stage for situations of joint work and for teacher collaboration in schools. Last, but not least, listening to the voices of retired teachers can serve to create empathy with other practitioners, and a sense of belonging to a vital, though vulnerable, profession.

SUMMARY COMMENTS

Different modes of introducing teachers' recollections, and the insights gained from their analysis, into teacher education and staff-development programs were discussed above. The professional events recalled and recorded by teachers are viewed as part of a case literature to be used in different contexts. According to Kagan (1993) classroom cases can be used in three different ways: as instructional materials in teacher education programs; as data for research on teacher cognition; and as catalysts for change and professional growth of teachers. Teachers' recollections can be used for all these purposes. Their use in teacher education is not limited to the enhancement of problem solving abilities of teachers. The recollected events provide an alternative way of infusing reality into teacher education. They can serve as catalysts for discussion and analysis of experience in various teaching situations. Recollected events of practice pertain to a richness of issues and reflect the complexities of professional lives of teachers. They provide insights into the history of education and the changing cultures of schools. Interpersonal relationships might play a major role in the events recorded by teachers, illuminating an important aspect of teaching that is often overlooked in teacher education programs.

Finally, teachers' collective remembering might become a regular feature of their work, contributing to the processes of joint planning and problem solving, and to the promotion of their professional identity.

APPENDIX: DESIGN OF THE STUDY ON MEMORY OF PROFESSIONAL EVENTS

METHODS OF STUDY

Research on memory of events has been conducted using a wide variety of methods. Cohen (1989) distinguishes between two main approaches: self-reports and naturalistic experiments. Self-reports rely on people's introspection into the way their memories function, the things they remember, their memory abilities, and so on. Different methods are used in order to stimulate introspection concerning memory of events. A common method is word-cueing. Respondents are presented with a list of cue words and are asked to report a memory that comes to mind (Rubin, Wetzler, and Nebes 1986). Sir Francis Galton used cue words for studying memory as far back as 1879. Soliciting self-reports may involve interviews, collecting autobiographical histories, diaries, or formal questionnaires about memory. Linton (1975), for instance, kept card-file records of daily events and tried to date a random sample of events once a month in order to figure out her rate of forgetting and the nature of items that were retained.

The validity of introspective evidence is discussed by Cohen (1989), who states that there has been a resurrection of introspective methods, though these are criticized by some researchers (Nisbett and Wilson 1977). Cohen concludes that "in spite of some reservations and difficulties, if self-report data derived from protocols and questionnaires are used and interpreted with care and caution they can be a valid and valuable source of information about memory in everyday life" (p. 12). The issue of autobiographical distortion has been considered as well by Baddeley (1990), who concludes that "much of our autobiographical recollection of the past is reasonably free of error, provided we stick to remembering the broad outline of events" (p. 310).

In recent psychological literature a debate about the relative merit of laboratory experiments and everyday memory research has occupied scholars involved in memory studies. Banaji and Crowder (1989) criticized the everyday memory approach, arguing that ecologically valid methods do not ensure generalizability of findings. Ceci and Bronfenbrenner (1991), Conway (1991), Loftus (1991), and Neisser (1991) responded to their criticism, providing examples of valid and productive naturalistic lines of research concerning everyday memory phenomena. Tulving (1991) and Klatzky (1991) propose a symbiosis of both approaches. Tulving (1991) states that "the science of memory is not a zero-sum game. There is no law that says that good facts or ideas can come out of one type of approach only if some other approach is suppressed. As in other fields of science, there is room for many different kinds of facts and ideas about memory and for many approaches" (p. 42)

VALIDITY OF FINDINGS

One concern that might have compromised to some extent the validity of our findings was the fact that respondents were not limited to a certain number of events they could produce. The median number of events was three, and thirteen of the forty-three teachers sample submitted only one event. Only four teachers submitted six or more events (two presented six events, one eight events, and one ten events). Because events recalled were of primary interest, the main unit of analysis was event (rather than teachers).

To evaluate the magnitude of bias that might have been introduced due to personal characteristics of the respondents, two checks were conducted. The distributions of events-per-respondent for those events in which each specific category was mentioned were examined. Overall, the median number of events per respondent dropped to one in most of the categories. Thus, related to the analyses of each content category, there seems to be no overrepresentation of specific respondents.

The second check was to randomly select one event for each respondent and run all the analyses with this one-event-per-respondent sample. The same overall patterns and directions of results as in the full events sample were replicated in general in this truncated sample.

Thus, although it is impossible to give an accurate estimate of the bias, we can state with a reasonable degree of confidence that the results reflect generalized patterns of relationship between the variables and only to a marginal degree the confounding of specific personal characteristics of response styles. It is our belief that the gain in terms of the wealth of the events, which was the source for the content analyses, by far exceeds the drawback of an unbalanced, and even slightly biased, formal statistical estimate. Furthermore, we did not wish to interfere with the flow of memories and did not want the respondents to impose on themselves any kind of personal censorship.

The relationships between various content categories and type of teacher, event period, and school population were examined using chi-square goodness-of-fit tests. Where individual teachers tended to contribute to more than one category, statistical tests were conducted separately for each category. For example, the relationship between the eight content categories and type of teacher were examined separately for each of the content categories. Thus, a 2 x 2 table was constructed in which each of the content categories (yes/no) was crossed with teacher type (school/kindergarten). Where individual teachers contributed to a single category only, one statistical test was conducted for all categories. For example, the four types of rules and principles were crossed with type of teacher to produce a 4 x 2 table, which was then analyzed via chi-square. Correlation between content categories and background variables of teachers was computed. These background variables were level of education, time since retirement, years on the job, and years of practice at the time of the recollected event.

The relationships between the affective quality of teachers' memories and tenure characteristics (e.g., years on the job, memory recency, and years since retirement) were examined using T-tests. Thus, means of the tenure variables were compared between the two groups of memories, positive and nonpositive.

REFERENCES

Alexander, D., D. Muir, and D. Chant. 1992. Interrogating stories: How teachers think they learned to teach. *Teaching and Teacher Education* 8, no. 1:59–68.

Anyon, J. 1981. Social class and school knowledge. *Curriculum Inquiry* 11, no. 1:3–42.

Baddeley, A. 1990. *Human memory: Theory and practice.* Hillsdale, N.J.: Erlbaum.

Ball, S. J., and I. F. Goodson, eds. 1985a. *Teachers' lives and careers.* Barcombe, Lewes, England, Falmer Press.

————, and I. F. Goodson. 1985b. Understanding teachers: Concepts and contexts. In *Teachers' lives and careers,* edited by S. J. Ball and I. F. Goodson, 1–26. Barcombe, Lewes, England, Falmer Press.

Banaji, M. R., and R. G. Crowder. 1989. The bankruptcy of everyday memory. *American Psychologist* 44, no. 9:1185–93.

Barclay, C. R. 1986. Schematization of autobiographical memory. In *Autobiographical memory,* edited by D. C. Rubin, 82–99. Cambridge: Cambridge University Press.

Bellah, R. N., R. Madsen, W. M. Sullivan, A. Swidler, and S. M. Tipton. 1985. *Habits of the heart: Individualism and commitment in American life.* Berkeley: University of California Press.

Booth, W. C. 1961. *The rhetoric of fiction.* Chicago: University of Chicago Press.

Bower, G. H., J. B. Black, and T. J. Turner. 1979. Scripts in text comprehension and memory. *Cognitive Psychology* 11, no. 1:177–220.

Brewer, W. F. 1986. What is autobiographical memory? In *Autobiographical memory*, edited by D. C. Rubin, 25–49. Cambridge: Cambridge University Press.

Britzman, D. P. 1986. Cultural myths in the making of a teacher: Biography and social structure in teacher education. *Harvard Educational Review* 56, no. 4:442–546.

Brown, R., and J. Kulik. 1977. Flashbulb memories. *Cognition* 5:73–99.

Bruner, J. 1986. *Actual minds, possible worlds.* Cambridge: Harvard University Press.

———. 1990. *Acts of meaning.* Cambridge: Harvard University Press.

Buchman, M. 1992. Figuring in the past: Thinking about teacher memories. Paper presented at the annual meeting of the American Educational Research Association, April, San Francisco.

Cantor, N., W. Mischel, and J. C. Schwartz. 1982. A prototype analysis of psychological situations. *Cognitive Psychology* 14:45–77.

Ceci, S. J., and U. Bronfenbrenner. 1991. On the demise of everyday memory. *American Psychologist* 46, no. 1:27–31.

Clandinin, D. J. 1986. *Classroom practice: Teacher images in action.* London: Falmer Press.

———, and F. M. Connelly. 1991. Narrative and story in practice and research. In *The reflective turn: Case studies in and on educational practice*, edited by D. A. Schon, 258–81. New York: Columbia University, Teachers College Press.

Cohen, G. 1989. *Memory in the real world.* Hillsdale N.J.: Erlbaum.

————, and D. Faulkner. 1988. Life span changes in autobiographical memory. In *Practical aspects of memory: Current research and issues*, edited by M. M. Gruenberg, P. E. Morris, and R. N. Sykes. Chichester, England: Wiley.

Coles, R. 1989. *The call of stories: Teaching and the moral imagination.* Boston: Houghton Mifflin.

Connelly, F. M., and D. J. Clandinin. 1985. Personal practical knolwedge and the modes for knowing: Relevance for teaching and learning. In *Learning and teaching the ways of knowing*, edited by E. Eisner, 2:174–98. Chicago: University of Chicago Press.

————, and D. J. Clandinin. 1986. On narrative method, personal philosophy, and narrative unities in the story of teaching. *Journal of Research in Science Teaching* 23, no. 4:283–310.

————, and D. J. Clandinin. 1990. Stories of experience and narrative inquiry. *Educational Researcher* 19, no. 5:2–14.

Conway, M. A. 1990. *Autobiographical memory: An introduction.* Philadelphia: Open University Press.

————. 1991. In defense of everyday memory. *American Psychologist* 46, no. 1:19–26.

Cornbleth, C. 1990. *Curriculum in context.* Barcombe Lewis, England: Falmer Press.

Dickson, P. 1978. *The official rules.* New York: Delacorte Press.

Douglas, M. 1986. *How institutions think.* London: Routledge & Kegan Paul.

Earle, W. 1956. Memory. *Review of Metaphysics* 10:3–27.

Eisner, E. W. 1991. *The enlightened eye*. New York: Macmillan.

Elbaz, F. 1981. The teacher's 'practical knolwedge': Report of a case study. *Curriculum Inquiry* 11, no. 1:43–71.

———. 1983. *Teacher thinking: A study of practical knowledge*. London: Croom Helm.

———. 1991. Research on teachers' knowledge: The evolution of a discourse. *Journal of Curriculum Studies* 23, no. 1:1–19.

Fitzgerald, J. M. 1988. Vivid memories and the reminiscence phenomenon: The role of a self narrative. *Human Development* 3:261–73.

Fivush, R., and E. A. Slackman. 1986. The acquisition and development of scripts. In *Event knowledge: Structure and function in development*, edited by K. Nelson, 71–96. Hillsdale, N.J.: Erlbaum.

Franklin, H. C., and J. H. Holding. 1977. Personal memories at different ages. *Quarterly Journal of Experimental Psychology* 29:527–32.

Freeman, D. 1991. 'To make the tacit explicit': Teacher education, emerging discourse and conceptions of teaching. *Teaching and Teacher Education* 7, no. 5/6:439–54.

Fullan, M. G. and S. Stiegelbauer. 1991: The new meaning of educational change. New York: Teachers College Press.

Galton, F. 1879. Psychometric experiments. *Brain* 2:144–62.

Gauthier, D. P. 1963. *Practical reasoning*. Oxford: Clarendon Press.

Goethals, G. R., and R. F. Reckman. 1982. Recalling previously held attitudes. In *Memory observed: Remembering in natural contexts*, edited by U. Neisser, 3–19. San Francisco: W. H. Freeman.

Goodson, I. F., ed. 1992. *Studying teachers' lives*. London: Routledge.

Greene, M. 1991. Foreword. In *Stories lives tell: Narrative and dialogue in education*, edited by C. Witherell and N. Noddings, ix–xi. New York: Teachers College Press.

Halbwachs, M. 1980. *The collective memory*. New York: Harper & Row.

Hansen, D. T. 1992. The emergence of a shared morality in a classroom. *Curriculum Inquiry* 22, no. 4:345–61.

Hayman, D., and E. S. Rabkin. 1974. *Form in fiction: An introduction to the analysis of narrative prose*. New York: St. Martin's Press.

Herbart, J. F. 1850–52. *Kurze Encyclopaedie der Philosophie aus pracktischen Gesichtpunkten entworfen*. Vol. 2. Leipzig: L. Voss.

Howarth, W. L. 1980. Some principles of autobiography. In *Autobiography: Essays theoretical and critical*, edited by J. Olney, 84–114. Originally published in *New Literary History* 5 (1974): 363–81.

Jackson, P. W. 1968. *Life in classrooms*. New York: Holt, Rinehart & Winston.

Kagan, D. M. 1993. Contexts for the use of classroom cases. *American Educational Research Journal* 30, no. 4:703–23.

Kelchterman, G. 1991. Teachers and their career story: A biographical perspective on professional development. Paper presented at the fifth conference of the International Study Association on Teacher Thinking, University of Surrey, Guilford, England, 23–27 September 1991.

Kihlstrom, J. F. 1981. On personality and memory. In *Personality, cognition and social interaction*, edited by N. Cantor and J. F. Kihlstrom, 123–49. Hillsdale, N.J.: Erlbaum.

Klatzky, R. L. 1991. Let's be friends. *American Psychologist* 46, no. 1:43–45.

Knowles, J. G., and D. Holt-Reynolds. 1991. Shaping pedagogies through personal histories in preservice teacher education. *Teachers College Record* 93, no. 1:87–113.

Leinhardt, G. 1990. Capturing craft knowledge in teaching. *Educational Researcher* 19, no. 2:18–24.

———, and J. G. Greeno. 1986. The cognitive skill of teaching. *Journal of Educational Psychology* 78:75–95.

———, C. Weidman, and K. M. Hammond. 1987. Introduction and integration of classroom routines by expert teachers. *Curriculum Inquiry* 17, no. 2:135–76.

Light, D. 1980. *Becoming psychiatrists: The professional transformation of self.* New York: W. W. Norton.

Linton, M. 1975. Memory for real-world events. In *Explorations in cognition,* edited by D. A. Norman and D. E. Rumelhart, 376–404. San Francisco: Freeman.

———. 1979. I remember it well. *Psychology Today,* July, 80–86.

———. 1982. Transformations of memory in everyday life. In *Memory observed: Remembering in natural contexts,* edited by U. Neisser, 77–91. San Francisco: W. H. Freeman.

———. 1986. Ways of searching and the contents of memory. In *Autobiographical memory,* edited by D. C. Rubin, 59–67. Cambridge: Cambridge University Press.

Little, J. W. 1990. The persistance of privacy: Autonomy and initiative in teachers' professional relations. *Teachers College Record* 91, no. 4:509–36.

Loftus, E. F. 1991. The glitter of everyday memory . . . and the gold. *American Psychologist* 46, no. 1:16–18.

Lortie, D. C. 1975. *School-teacher: A sociological study.* Chicago: University of Chicago Press.

Lucariello, J., and A. Rifkin. 1986. Event representation as the basis for categorical knowledge. In *Event knowledge: Structure and function in development,* edited by K. Nelson, 189–209. Hillsdale, N.J.: Erlbaum.

Mandler, J. M. 1979. Categorical and schematic organization in memory. In *Memory organization and structure,* edited by C. R. Puff, 259–99. New York: Academic Press.

Matlin, M., and D. Stang. 1978. *The Pollyanna principle: Selectivity in language, memory and thought.* Cambridge, Mass.: Schenckman.

McCloskey, M., and K. Bigler. 1980. Focused memory search in fact retrieval. *Memory and Cognition* 8:253–64.

Meyerhof, B. 1986. Life not death in Venice: It's second life. In *The anthropology of experience,* edited by V. W. Turner and E. M. Bruner, 261–88. Urbana: University of Illinois Press.

Middleton, D., and D. Edwards, eds. 1990*a*. *Collective Remembering.* London: Sage.

———, and D. Edwards, eds. 1990*b*. Introduction. In *Collective remembering,* edited by D. Middleton and D. Edwards, 1–22. London: Sage.

Neisser, U. 1982a. Memory: What are the important questions? In *Memory observed: Remembering in natural contexts,* edited by U. Neisser, 3–19. San Francisco: W. H. Freeman.

———. 1982b. Snapshots or benchmarks? In *Memory observed: Remembering in natural contexts,* edited by U. Neisser, 77–91. San Francisco: W. H. Freeman.

———. 1986. Nested structure in autobiographical memory. In *Autobiographical memory,* edited by D. C. Rubin, 71–81. Cambridge: Cambridge University Press.

————. 1991. A case of misplaced nostalgia. *American Psychologist* 46, no. 1:34–36.

Nelson, K. 1986. Event knowledge and cognitive development. In *Event knowledge: Structure and function in development*, edited by K. Nelson, 1–19. Hillsdale, N.J.: Erlbaum.

————, and J. Gruendel. 1981. Generalized event representations: Basic building blocks of cognitive development. In *Advances in developmental psychology*, edited by M. E. Lamb and A. L. Brown. Hillsdale, N.J.: Erlbaum.

Nigro, G., and U. Neisser. 1983. Point of view in personal memories. *Cognitive Psychology* 15:467–82.

Nir, R. 1984. *Language, medium and message* [in Hebrew]. Jerusalem: Posner.

Nisbett, R. E., and T. D. Wilson. 1977. Telling more than we can know: Verbal reports on mental processes. *Psychological Review* 84:231–59.

Noddings, N. 1984. *Caring*. Berkeley: University of California Press.

————, and C. Witherell. 1991. Themes remembered and foreseen. In *Stories lives tell: Narrative and dialogue in education*, edited by C. Witherell and N. Noddings, 279–80. New York: Teachers College Press.

Orr, J. E. 1990. Sharing knowledge, celebrating identity: Community memory in a service culture. In *Collective remembering*, edited by D. Middleton and D. Edwards, 169–89. London: Sage.

Pillemer, D. B., L. R. Goldsmith, A. T. Panter, and S. H. White. 1988. Very long-term memories of the first year in college. *Journal of Experimental Psychology: Learning, Memory and Cognition* 14:709–15.

Rabin, E. 1975. *Schattenbilder*. Givatayim: Massada.

Reiser, B. J., J. B. Black, and P. Kalamanides. 1986. Strategic memory search processes. In *Autobiographical memory*, edited by D. C. Rubin, 100–21. Cambridge: Cambridge University Press.

Robinson, J. A. 1976. Sampling autobiographical memory. *Cognitive Psychology* 8:578–95.

———. 1986. Autobiographical memory: A historical prologue. In *Autobiographical memory*, edited by D. C. Rubin, 25–49. Cambridge: Cambridge University Press.

Rosenholtz, S. J. 1991. *Teachers' workplace*. New York: Teachers College Press.

Ross, J. A., and E. M. Regan. 1993. Sharing professional experience: Its impact on professional development. *Teaching and Teacher Education* 9, no. 1:91–106.

Rowe, M. B. 1974. Relation of wait-time and rewards to the development of language, logic and fate control. Part II: Rewards. *Journal of Research in Science Teaching* 11, no. 4:291–308.

Rubin, D. C., and M. Kozin. 1984. Vivid memories. *Cognition* 16:81–95.

———, G. E. Wetzler, and R. D. Nebes. 1986. Autobiographical memory across the life span. In *Autobiographical memory*, edited by D. C. Rubin, 202–21. Cambridge: Cambridge University Press.

Russell, T., and H. Munby. 1991. Reframing: The role of experience in developing teachers' professional knowledge. In *The reflective turn: Case studies in and on educational practice*, edited by D. A. Schon, New York: Teachers College Press.

Sarason, S. B. 1971. *The culture of the school and the problem of change*. Boston: Allyn & Bacon.

Schank, R. C. 1982. *Dynamic memory*. Cambridge: Cambridge University Press.

————, and R. P. Abelson. 1977. *Scripts, plans, goals and understanding.* Hillsdale, N.J.: Erlbaum.

Schubert, W. H. 1992. Our journeys into teaching: Remembering the past. In *Teacher lore: Learning from our own experience,* edited by W. H. Schubert and W. C. Ayers, 3–10. New York: Longman.

————, and W. C. Ayers, eds. 1992. *Teacher Lore: Learning from our own experience.* New York: Longman.

Shulman, J. H., ed. 1992. *Case methods in teacher education.* New York: Teachers College Press.

Shulman, L. S. 1986. Those who understand: Knowledge growth in teaching. *Educational Researcher* 15, no. 2:4–17.

————. 1987. Knowledge and teaching: Foundations of the new reform. *Harvard Educational Review* 57, no. 1:1–22.

Sikes, P. J. 1985. The life cycle of the teacher. In *Teachers' lives and careers,* edited by S. J. Ball and J. F. Goodson, 27–60. Barcombe Lewes, England: Falmer Press.

Slackman, E. A., J. A. Hudson, and R. Fivush. (1986). Actions, actors, links and goals: The structure of children's event representation. In *Event knowledge: Structure and function in development,* edited by K. Nelson, 47–69. Hillsdale, N.J.: Erlbaum.

Spence, D. P. 1982. *Narrative truth and historical truth: Meaning and interpretation in psychoanalysis.* New York: Norton.

Stein, N. L., and S. Goldman. 1979. *Children's knowledge about social situations.* Center for the study of Reading Technical Report, 147. Urbana: University of Illinois.

Stenhouse, L. 1979. Case study in comparative education: Particularity and generalisation. *Comparative Education* 15, no. 1:5–10.

Sternberg, M. 1974. What is exposition: An essay in temporal delimitation. In *The theory of the novel: New essays*, edited by J. Halperin, 25–70. New York: Oxford University Press.

Tulving, E. 1972. Episodic and semantic memory. In *Organization of memory*, edited by E. Tulving and W. Donaldson, 381–403. New York: Academic Press.

———. 1991. Memory research is not a zero-sum game. *American Psychologist* 46, no. 1:41–42.

Van Dijk, T. A. 1980. *Text and context: Explorations in the semantics and pragmatics of discourse*. London: Longman.

Wagenaar, W. A. 1986. My memory: A study of autobiographical memory over six years. *Cognitive Psychology* 18:226–52.

White, R. Y. 1982. Memory for personal events. *Human Learning* 1:171–83.

Woods, P. 1987. Life histories and teacher knowledge. In *Educating teachers: Changing the nature of pedagogical knowledge*, edited by J. Smyth, 121–35. London: Falmer Press.

Wyer, R. S., and T. K. Scrull. 1989. *Memory and cognition in its social context*. Hillsdale, N.J.: Erlbaum.

Zerubavel, E. 1981. *Hidden Rhythms*. Chicago: University of Chicago Press.

INDEX